CYBER POLICY IN CHINA ———

D1188987

China Today series

CYBER POLICY
IN CHINA

Greg Austin

polity

First published in 2014 by Polity Press

Polity Press
65 Bridge Street
Cambridge CB2 1UR, UK

Polity Press
350 Main Street
Malden, MA 02148, USA

ISBN-13: 978-0-7456-6979-3
ISBN-13: 978-0-7456-6980-9 (pb)

A catalogue record for this book is available from the British Library.

Typeset in 11.5 on 15 pt Adobe Jenson Pro
by Toppan Best-set Premedia Limited
Printed and bound in Great Britain by Clays Ltd, St Ives PLC

The publisher has used its best endeavours to ensure that the URLs for external websites referred to in this book are correct and active at the time of going to press. However, the publisher has no responsibility for the websites and can make no guarantee that a site will remain live or that the content is or will remain appropriate.

Every effort has been made to trace all copyright holders, but if any have been inadvertently overlooked the publisher will be pleased to include any necessary credits in any subsequent reprint or edition.

For further information on Polity, visit our website: www.politybooks.com

This book is dedicated to Angelica and Elvira.

Contents

Tables

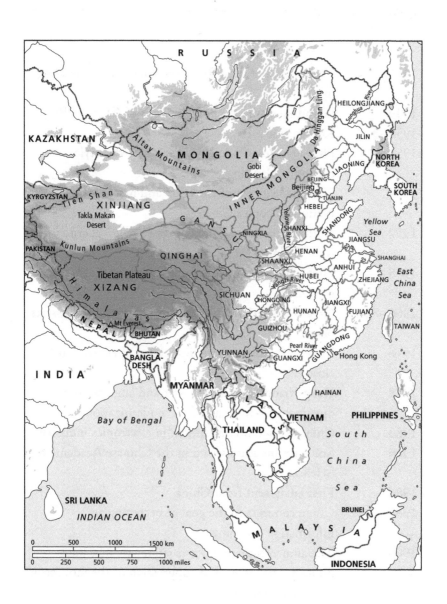

Chronology

1911	Chinese Republican Revolution and fall of the Qing dynasty
1949	Founding of the People's Republic of China (PRC)
1950–3	Korean War
1953–7	First Five-Year Plan; PRC adopts Soviet-style economic planning
1954	First constitution of the PRC and first meeting of the National People's Congress
1957	Anti-rightist campaign suppresses political criticism of Mao Zedong
1958	First Chinese computer built, based on designs from the USSR
1966–76	Great Proletarian Cultural Revolution; Mao reasserts power
1976	Mao dies; most universities reopen after ten years' closure
1978	Deng Xiaoping rises to power and launches the opening up, reform and four modernizations
1983	China accelerates investment in electronics industry
1985	Software Institute set up in the Chinese Academy of Sciences
1986	First email sent from China
1987	China commits to the goal of becoming an information economy
1989	Tiananmen Square protests culminate in 4 June military crackdown and suppression of the movement for science and democracy

1990	First Chinese-made PC launched in the domestic market
1992	US National Science Foundation rebuffs China's first request for public access to the internet; Deng Xiaoping's Southern Inspection Tour re-energizes economic reforms
1993–2005	Jiang Zemin takes Deng's place as paramount leader and continues economic growth agenda
1994	Competition in mobile phones introduced with establishment of Unicom
1995	Internet and world wide web come to the Chinese public
1996	State-owned Great Wall Technology Group set up
1997	Chinese telecoms companies part privatize on the New York Stock Exchange
1998	Ministry of Information Industry set up; Chinese web portals Sina and Sohu open
1999	China suppresses Falun Gong; China agrees tough terms that will enable it to join the World Trade Organization; Yahoo! in China; eBay clone EachNet set up
2000	Chinese Communist Party (CCP) general secretary Jiang Zemin commits China publicly to the goal of becoming an information society
2002	Microsoft is first foreign company admitted to China Software Association
2002–12	Hu Jintao is general secretary of the CCP and president of China from 2003
2003	China changes military doctrine to emphasize informatization

2005   Sina launches a blog capability; first internet TV licence issued

2006   Long-term plan for national informatization to 2020 launched

2008   New super-ministry of industry and information technology is set up

2009   China bans Twitter and Skype

2010   China's armed forces set up a leading group on informatization

2011   Obama says United States is facing another 'Sputnik moment', referencing cyber espionage by China

2012   Reports of cyber surveillance of China's leaders by its own police; Xi Jinping is general secretary of the CCP, and president of China from 2013

2013   New crackdown on anti-CCP information, the constitution movement and journalists

2014   Xi Jinping is first general secretary of CCP to take direct control of the leadership group on informatization, led since 2001 by the premier

Preface

The internet came to the public in China in 1995. Twenty years later, China has the biggest population of netizens in the world; it has become the world's biggest producer of desktop computers; and two of its telecommunications equipment providers are among the world's largest. Is China on a pathway to dominance in cyberspace? It could be. Yet, as impressive as those few manifestations of China's digital prowess are, they can be viewed as part of a much bigger canvas – the idea of an information society. This concept predates the creation of the internet by several decades and is defined by many features much more wide-ranging in scope than the sorts of measures just mentioned.

The idea of an information society evolved from an earlier concept of 'information economy' or 'knowledge economy'. In 1962, economist Fritz Machlup estimated for the first time the monetary value of knowledge production in the United States and how this form of production had transformed the economy (Machlup 1962). By the early 1970s, various commentaries on his work had elaborated on the concept of the 'knowledge economy' and 'information economy', portending an information revolution every bit as transformative in social and political terms as the industrial revolution.

The world was now in an information age. The transformative effect of the new age was seen early on as extending beyond the industrial and the economic domains to reach the very moral fabric of society. Norbert Wiener (1964) penned a short work appropriately titled *God & Golem, Inc.*, with the subtitle 'A Comment on Certain Points where Cybernetics Impinges on Religion'. Bell (1976) predicted that the information revolution would be the catalyst for a post-industrial society and that information exchange would become the basis of all economic and social exchange. One of the most insightful antecedents, however, was probably Masuda (1981 [1980]), who coined the word 'computopia', thereby anticipating the comprehensive and profound effects of information technologies and their use. Masuda foreshadowed 'the realisation of a society that brings about a general flourishing state of human intellectual creativity, instead of affluent material consumption'. He also anticipated e-democracy, the globalization of a new renaissance, a shattering of previous conceptions of privacy, the emergence of a new concept of time-value, and a new intensity in system innovation – all premised on the complete objectification and commodification of information.

By the early 1990s, the concept of the information society had become globally prominent as an important goal of national and international policy. In 2000, China's leaders embraced the goal of an information society in a series of policy statements and administrative acts that are documented later. By 2002 and 2003, the United Nations (UN) system got behind the goal and convened the World Summit on the Information Society (WSIS). There was one basic reason. The advent of the information society was seen as global in scope and revolutionary in its impact on state power. The vision accepted by most countries participating in the WSIS, including China, was a grand vision of society transformed by the material, intellectual and social attributes of information technologies and the knowledge economy. The ideal has been described by the UN as a society 'where everyone can create, access, utilise and share information and knowledge' to 'achieve their full potential' in 'improving their quality of life' (UN Docs WSIS-03/GENEVA/DOC/4-E 12 December 2003). The idea in this formulation is 'people-centred'.

In Chinese, information society is most often rendered as *xìnxī shèhuì* (信息社会). A common substitute for the term 'information society' is the term *xìnxīhuà* (信息化), which can be translated as 'informatization'. It is often used in Chinese sources (as in English ones) to contrast with industrialization (*chănyèhuà* or *gōngyèhuà*) as a period in social and economic history. In China, informatization has been defined as 'the historical process, during which information technology is fully used, information resources are developed and utilized, the exchange of information and knowledge sharing are promoted, the quality of economic growth is improved, and the transformation of economic and social development is promoted' (Central Committee and State Council 2006). It is broadly cognate with the Chinese government's concept of an information society, though it could be interpreted as less people-centred than the UN vision and more in the mould of the materialist and technocratic traditions that Chinese Communists have preferred. The idea of an information society cuts across a wide sweep of policy (politics, culture, art, economy, industry, education, science, technology, diplomacy and security).

The analysis here started as an effort to evaluate China's progress towards its goal of becoming an advanced information society. Within a short time, given China's political system, I came to see the preferences of the country's leaders as a key determinant and a worthy subject of study. What do Chinese leaders actually want from the information society and what dilemmas have they confronted in framing their policies? This then led me to look more closely at their political values – their ethics – not least because Chinese figures prominent in informatization policy made this connection themselves, as had statements from many delegations to the WSIS.

On the assumption that outcomes in the information society are ethically determined, the analytical framework used in the book revolves around ideal policy values for achieving an advanced information society. This framework is derived from a study of ethics. Thus, the analysis is not presented as a work in social science (be that political science, political economy, industry policy or strategic studies). It is a more simple effort to situate the values of China's leaders within an ethical framework implied by their acceptance of the ambition to become an advanced information society. Since the analysis is intended to give a sense of the trajectory of China's ambition (where has it come from and the likely timeline for achieving the goal), it relies on a chronological treatment in each section.

Chapter 1 sets the scene for later chapters. It offers an introduction of China's ambition to become an advanced information society, identifying the year 2000 as the time when the leaders first adopted the information society ambition in policy. The chapter then sets out the framework of nine ideal policy values needed for an information society. Chapter 2 provides a short interpretative overview of China's information society prehistory in the period from 1949 to 1999. It shows how the leaders worked hard for almost three decades to suppress the emergence of an information society. Then, after 1978, they had to struggle to reverse the worst effects of that repression, opening up gradually to the idea of an information economy and later the idea of an information society. The following chapters look more closely at the leaders' policy values in the fifteen years since the start of this century, comparing them with the ideal values. Each of chapters 3, 4 and 5 takes three of the nine ideal values in turn, looking at them from the Chinese leaders' perspective. Thus, these chapters are titled 'e-Democracy i-Dictatorship', 'Innovative Information Economy', and 'Security in the Global Infosphere'. As already suggested, chapters 2–5 blend thematic issues with a chronological presentation. The presentation of developments sequentially by year is intentional and essential. Without it, the reader would not get a sense of the trajectory of China's information society policy. How quickly and how nimbly have its leaders moved? How well and how enthusiastically have they adjusted to opportunity or to failure? Are they on schedule to meet their targets? A short conclusion (chapter 6) looks at the feedback effect between these three domains of policy and the associated ideal policy values, and how that positions China going forward.

Acknowledgements

I would like to thank Professor Li Maosen and the Ethics Centre of the Department of Philosophy at Renmin University for helping me understand during my stay there the Chinese view of the contours of information ethics and moral education. This book debates that Chinese view and I alone am responsible for that. It is to the credit of the university and China that I was received so warmly while conducting this research. I would also like to thank Professor Luciano Floridi of Oxford University for orienting my understanding of the information age as a set of ethical problems. I owe a debt to Professor Mervyn Frost of King's College London for showing me the centrality of ethical contest in international affairs and how it can be (and has to be) distinguished from social science. I am indebted to the Department of War Studies at King's College for my time there as a Visiting Senior Fellow while I researched and wrote this book. Dr Thomas Rid provided important support. The EastWest Institute, particularly John Mroz, provided a unique environment for policy debates on the issues.

The manuscript has been improved as the result of critical review by two anonymous colleagues who identified important gaps or inconsistencies in the draft. I am grateful to Eric Cappon, who acted as the surrogate 'general reader' at the final stage to test the readability of the manuscript for its target audience. The quality of the manuscript has been dramatically enhanced through advice from Louise Knight at Polity and at an earlier stage from Kay Templeton in Sydney. Pascal Porcheron at Polity made the finishing touches. Fiona Sewell undertook a most thorough and thoughtful final edit. Special thanks to my wife Kay for continued support.

Abbreviations

At the request of the publisher, this list omits commonly understood abbreviations from international relations (such as UN for the United Nations), common abbreviations from the field of information society policy (such as ICT for information and communications technology) and abbreviations that only occur within a couple of pages of first mention.

ACSI	Advisory Committee for State Informatization
APEC	Asia-Pacific Economic Cooperation
ASEAN	Association of Southeast Asian Nations
CAS	Chinese Academy of Sciences
CASS	Chinese Academy of Social Sciences
CCP	Chinese Communist Party
CERNET	China Education and Research Network
CMC	Central Military Commission
CNCERT	National Computer Network Emergency Response Technical Team Coordination Center
CNNIC	China Internet Network Information Center
CPLC	Central Political and Legal Commission
CPPCC	Chinese People's Political Consultative Conference
CUST	China University of Science and Technology
FOI	freedom of information
ICANN	Internet Corporation for Assigned Names and Numbers
IPR	intellectual property rights
IPv6	Internet Protocol version 6
ISP	internet service provider
ITU	International Telecommunication Union
IW	information warfare

KIP	Knowledge Innovation Programme
MEI	Ministry of Electronics Industry
MII	Ministry of Information Industry
MIIT	Ministry of Industry and Information Technology
MLP	Medium and Long-Term Development Plan for Science and Technology 2006–20
MPS	Ministry of Public Security
MSS	Ministry of State Security
NIP	National Informatization Plan
NPC	National People's Congress
NRI	Network Readiness Index
OGI	Open Government Initiative
PBoC	People's Bank of China
PLA	People's Liberation Army
PRC	People's Republic of China
PSC	Politburo Standing Committee
ROC	Republic of China
SCITO	State Council Informatization Office
SILG	State Informatization Leading Group
SIPO	State Intellectual Property Office
SOE	state-owned enterprise
WEF	World Economic Forum
WSIS	World Summit on the Information Society

1 | China's Cyber Ambition ───────

China's political leaders have expressed a vision of making the country into a world-class information society. This involves the widespread application in the economy and the society of advanced technologies in information processing and its exploitation, based on a pervasive communications infrastructure. Jiang Zemin, former general secretary of the Communist Party, laid out this general vision in at least three major speeches in Beijing in 2000: in addressing Communist Party members attending the National People's Congress (NPC) and the Chinese People's Political Consultative Conference (CPPCC) on 3 March; in welcoming remarks at the opening of the 16th World Computer Congress on 21 August; and in a speech to a meeting of the Central Military Commission (CMC) on 11 December (see Jiang 2010). Wen Jiabao, former premier, saw the ambition as a 'mega-trend for development in the contemporary world, a major force in promoting economic and social development and reform' (www.gov.cn 04/11/2005). According to a former senior adviser, the country's leaders were seeing informatization as the 'main power driving the country's overall economic and social development' (Qu 2010).

The Chinese delegate to one of the preparatory meetings of the World Summit on the Information Society (WSIS) signalled China's position as follows (Sha 2002). Countries with different social systems and cultural traditions will handle the transition to an information society differently. Information infrastructure will be the foundation of future economic progress but it is weak in developing countries (among which China counted itself). Managing the transition, he said, would demand policy responses across a broad front in line with national conditions (macroeconomic control, market regulation policies, balancing technological development and market growth, avoiding market risks and innovative financing mechanisms). The security of the state would be a high priority. The developed countries should have an obligation to transfer technologies and develop the human resources of developing countries (to bridge the digital divide). The private sector and civil society would be important drivers, but in framing international responses, the governments should be in the lead.

The earliest systematic and public presentation of the Chinese leadership view did not come until six years later, in the National Informatization Plan (NIP) 2006–20 (Central Committee and State Council 2006). The State Informatization Leading Group (SILG), chaired by the premier and comprising several colleagues from the Politburo of the Chinese Communist Party (CCP), had approved the NIP in principle in November 2005. There had been an informatization strategy in the 2001–5 Five-Year Plan but it was largely oriented towards information technology narrowly defined, rather than towards the information society ambition touted by its leaders at the time (see chapter 4 for more detail). The main lines of the NIP 2006–20, which are set out in table 1.1, covered a broad sweep of policy consistent with the transformational vision of an information society.

In China, the concept of an information society (like the term 'harmonious society' or 'patriotic society') differs according to the person using the term or even the occasion on which one person uses it. There can be no rigid definition of informatization or the information society. At a basic level, the terms suggest a prioritization of the value placed upon information and how it is used, especially through advanced technologies, products and networks. But, as outlined in this book, the intensity and scope of China's ambition, as documented in many places,

Table 1.1: Priorities of the NIP, 2006–2020

- promote the information society
- promote economic information
- strengthen the development and utilization of information resources
- implement e-government
- build advanced internet culture
- improve the integration of information infrastructure
- improve the competitiveness of the information technology (IT) industry
- build a national information security system
- improve national capacity by creating a pool of IT personnel
- improve policy and research
- improve investment and financing policies
- promote an IT legal system
- strengthen international exchanges and cooperation in IT
- improve the promotion of informatization

---

suggest that the high-end version – radically transformative effect – is what at least some of the leaders had in mind.

One estimate of the scale of social and political transformation still ahead for China can be found in the Chinese Academy of Sciences (CAS) report *Information Science and Technology in China: A Roadmap to 2050* (Li Guojie 2011). Its plan is staggeringly ambitious and complex. It is based on a commitment to approaching the frontiers of science, economics and social organization in the sphere of informatization by 2050. The report comes close to arguing for a new set of political values in order to make the necessary transition. While much of the argument about political change in China is made disparately and buried somewhat in the technical jargon, the Executive Summary gives a slightly clearer set of markers. Some sound simply technocratic, but as later discussion in the report suggests, they are also deeply political. They are clearly more humanistic (people-centred) than the summary points in table 1.1 from the NIP 2006–20. The CAS report says that the national information systems – presumably meaning in politics, science and the economy – need to:

- be user oriented
- be ubiquitous
- offer 'convenient' access to information
- provide the ability for people to 'more effectively cooperate'
- create opportunities for a 'higher quality of life'
- be seen as a human and social phenomenon rather just as a technological enabler
- operate 'free from monopoly'
- have Chinese characteristics through an expansion of Chinese language web content
- meet national security needs
- allow for the construction of a harmonious society.

Towards the end of the report, in a short subsection called 'social computing', which appears at first glance to have only a limited technical meaning, the authors open up the political question without answering it. They say 'social computing research and applications have become an urgent agenda for ensuring national security and harmonious development'. While observing the desirable growth of people-to-people networking, they note that 'the entire community realizes that these new technologies will profoundly affect the structure, organisation and activity patterns of future society'. We might reasonably interpret this to mean the political system. The changes will be unpredictable, the report says, but will need to be managed. The authors call for urgent adoption of an overarching 'theory of social computing'. This could be interpreted to mean new rules for less government intervention in cyberspace and in network supervision – what is referred to in the report's Executive Summary as the 'monopoly' over the information networks. The document would have been discussed with and approved by senior Communist Party officials, since the political implications of the objectives highlighted here are significant.

By November 2013, the leaders had endorsed a set of sixty reform measures (or principles) at a plenum of the Central Committee of the CCP (Central Committee 2013). Without using the term 'informatization' or 'information society', many of these measures called for the establishment of relevant information systems and their exploitation as an underpinning of national advance. For example, the leadership made demands for:

- more rapid movement to an innovative society
- national uniform economic accounting systems and 'other basic data for the entire society'
- more open information on budgets and finance for state-owned enterprises (SOEs)
- more interdepartmental information sharing
- acceleration of the perfection of leading structures for internet management
- guarantees for the security of the national network and of information
- publication of environmental information in a timely manner
- full utilization of informatized means to stimulate balanced distribution of high-quality healthcare resources
- perfection of leadership systems and the unified management of information assets and technologies in the armed forces.

Reading these 2013 priorities, with a new leadership installed only one year previously, it is difficult to escape the conclusion that the strength of leadership commitment to informatization as an overarching and all-encompassing policy had weakened somewhat. This was further evident in December 2013 when the Politburo Standing Committee (PSC) singled out agriculture as the weakest of the 'four pursuits': industrialization, informatization, urbanization and agriculture. This was a novel framing suggestive of a downgrading of the informatization goal over previous years away from being the overall driver of economic prosperity and social organization.

HOW CHINA HAS FARED

Since 2000, China's gains against its informatization ambition have been impressive. To illustrate the point, we can take five dimensions of an information society as examples. In industry, from a very low (negligible) base three decades earlier, China was claiming by 2009 to have the biggest IT industry in the world and to be ranked first in production of many related items (Jiang 2010). On the social front, there has been explosive growth in the exchange and use of information, raw and processed, through many different internet-based systems or through mobile computing: news sites like Sina, microblogs like Sina Weibo, YouTube lookalikes Tudou.com and youku.com, personal meeting sites (such as Mimiwang.com.cn), business networking sites (such as 365ju.com) and the Flickr lookalike Youpoo. In scientific research on information technologies, China is making great strides, exemplified by the news in November 2012 that a group of six Chinese scientists were claiming the 'first teleportation between two remote macroscopic objects', a process that provides a building block for the development of quantum networks and distributed quantum computing (Bao et al. 2012). In the field of internet architecture, China has taken a leading role in the development of an Internet Protocol version 6 (IPv6). In the security sphere, China has created the largest and most effective network of internet monitors and censors in the world and it is credited with spectacular successes in cyber espionage against the United States and other countries.

As a counterpoint to these and similar successes, China's government and informatization specialists see them as niche gains that are ahead of the play in terms of China's march towards an information society. An article published in 2012 reported the low standing of China in international comparisons of informatization, in both Chinese indexes and international indexes (Chao et al. 2012). The CAS *Roadmap to 2050* (Li Guojie 2011) made similar observations. A similar view can be found in non-Chinese sources, such as the 2013 Network Readiness Index (NRI) of the World Economic Forum (WEF), which had China sitting at 58th in world rankings for its use of information technologies to advance its national competitiveness and its citizens' lives (WEF and INSEAD 2013). China had slipped to that position from 36th in the 2011 rankings via 51st in 2012 (WEF and INSEAD 2012, 2011). The NRI provides an indexed comparison of the 'network readiness' of nearly 200 countries using a wide range of indicators. In the 2001–2 report, China ranked 64th (Kirkman et al. 2002). The United States, Japan, Singapore, Taiwan, South Korea and Malaysia are all ahead of China in the 2013 NRI.

The NRI gives only a partial picture of China in the cyber world, but it mirrors quite critical sentiment within the country about its weak position relative to others. The slippage by China in global informatization rankings has been specifically addressed by Chinese specialists (Chao et al. 2012). While these authors offered some critique of three indexes including the NRI, they also concluded that the 'analysis of the reasons for the rankings change contributes to an objective assessment of China's position in the global informa-tion wave'. Such analysis, the authors said, would 'help promote the rapid and healthy development' of the country's information technology.

A LEADERSHIP VIEW

Many constituencies have been involved in setting policy for China's information society, more so since 2000 than previously. These include the CCP, government officials (the technocrats), the armed forces, internal security agencies, business leaders, scholars, civil society, the media, religious groups and bloggers. Foreign companies, foreign governments and foreign civil society actors, alongside international organizations, have also played a highly visible role. There is now a cacophony of views in China on most policy subjects and the internet has transformed the character of the political dialogue on informatization policy. As the number of stakeholders has increased, opinions have become highly pluralized, and all ideas, including extreme right and left, can be widely disseminated (subject to post-publication censorship). Yet, while the internet may have opened up the dialogue massively, it has not broken the power of the one-party state. Leadership views remain decisive in most areas of policy even though their ability to enforce their directives has been weakened by the pluralization of society.

There is insufficient evidence to be able to assess what individual political leaders in China actually believe about anything. That is due in part to the fact that, in all political systems, leaders are obliged to temper personal values according to the political exigencies of the day. The actions of an individual leader therefore do not necessarily provide direct evidence of her or his views. Lack of insight into the personal views of this or that leader in China is also due in part to the closed nature of its political system, the lack of reporting on what the leaders say in private, and the high political cost for its leaders of being seen to be diverging from the leadership consensus. So, in focusing on the leaders, this book acknowledges that it is setting aside, for the purposes of argument, a detailed study of the many 'intervening variables' of political process (Duan 2012). The book is in effect hypothesizing a leadership view based on the net effect of their actions and statements in respect of four interrelated processes: awareness building and vision setting; resource mobilization; enhancing institutional performance; and setting trends (Duan 2012).

In looking at outcomes as evidence of leadership views, we need to acknowledge that a leader by himself or herself achieves nothing. Policy is shaped and executed (or diluted) by those lower in the hierarchy. This process of surrogate leadership by the second and third tier of leadership has been particularly evident in information society policy in China. The way in which China's leaders have come to their decisions at each milestone en route to this goal has in large part been due to a class of people (some leaders but mostly technocrats, scholars, bureaucrats and more recently entrepreneurs) who were able to bridge between an inherently conservative and isolationist CCP and the outside world, not just in information technology, but also in economic policy areas such as decentralization and competitiveness (Duan 2012).

IDEAL VALUES FOR INFORMATION SOCIETY POLICY

There are many different views on what constitutes an information society and the appropriate policies for achieving it. In terms of practical policy, most countries have developed some sort of national-level plan, with some having started several decades ago, and all having variations from others according to national conditions and political priorities. As internationalization of the issue took hold after the turn of the century, a number of global guides, templates or indexes were set in place.

China set up its own informatization index in 2000 on the instructions of the SILG. They were determined to track progress of their informatization ambition against a national baseline as well against international comparisons. Research sources used for creating the index included similar assessment tools from Japan, Asia-Pacific Economic Cooperation (APEC), the European Union, Seattle city government and the International Telecommunication Union (ITU)

(Xu 2004). Yet even these sources were largely about the information technologies, rather than a broader social concept of informatization. Around 2007, the CCP committee of the CAS approved a science-led assessment of China's informatization, including an alternative index that started collecting data in 2008. It too focused less on the social aspects and more on the technical aspects (information security, informatization construction, informatization services and informatization promotion).

Outside China, in 2002, the WEF partnered with the Center for International Development at Harvard University to produce *The Global Information Technology Report 2001–2002: Readiness for the Networked World*, described by the editors as the 'most comprehensive documentation to date of how ICTs are being used around the world' (Kirkman et al. 2002). One purpose of the report, which has become a widely referenced annual publication (cited earlier), was to address the 'major opportunities and obstacles that global leaders face as they try to more fully participate in the Networked World'. The WSIS Geneva Action Plan agreed in December 2003 provides a comprehensive view of the character of an information society, while allowing for national variation (www.itu.org/wsis). Of special note is that it calls out the ethical, human rights and political aspects as well as economic and social development. In 2004, the United Nations Conference on Trade and Development (UNCTAD) set up the Partnership on Measuring ICT for Development 'as an international, multistakeholder initiative to improve the availability and quality of ICT data and indicators, particularly in developing countries' (*measuring-ict. unctad.org*). The ITU has a series of annual publications, *Measuring the Information Society*, dating back to 2007 (see ITU 2013), which grew out of earlier work on an ICT opportunity index.

At the scholarly level, there is a vast literature on the information society. Most notably, there are studies that critique the transformative pretensions of the information society ambition, and others that embrace it, going so far as to elucidate a new philosophy of the information age. In the first group, one might mention Frank Webster's *Theories of the Information Society* (2006). He wisely questions the idea that the information society is a dominant new paradigm that sweeps other modes of analysis and social relationship aside. He leaves the reader believing that the idea of the information society is merely a way of instrumentalizing certain aspects of social change and does not in itself redefine our reality. He prefers the 'idea of an informatization of life which stems from the continuity of established forces'.

Robert Hassan's *The Information Society* (2008) takes on the 'boosters' and critics of the information society idea, with a political economy perspective that is persuasive. He rests his case on the conjunction between neo-liberal globalization (capitalism) and the 'revolution in the development and application of computer-based technologies'. He suggests that the information society has created not just 'pathways of possibility' but also a 'democratic vacuum' that will need to find a new controlling impulse from within, or 'we will continue to accelerate towards destinations unknown'. Manuel Castells, in his *Networks of Outrage and Hope* (2012), offers the view that politics has been forever transformed in certain dimensions, for better and for worse, by the new information technologies and their mass application, especially in social media forms. He concludes with an observation about 'the uncertainty of an uncharted process of political change' as the main political force unleashed by mass actions supported by modern social media. He sees political power resting with the established institutions, especially if they can co-opt the more popular themes of activists. But he warns that the more citizens can convey their messages, the more their consciousness is raised, and 'the more the public sphere becomes a contest terrain, and the lesser will be the politicians' capacity to integrate demands and claims'.

On the philosophy, Luciano Floridi at Oxford University is one of the leading scholars, with his 2013 volume, *The Ethics of Information*, providing deep insights into the moral implications of the information age. Such works debate an issue of the highest relevance to Chinese leadership choices on this subject. Just how transformative is the information society? Is it indeed revolutionary and overarching, affecting everything in fundamental ways? Or is it just another new factor that leaders must address alongside traditional preoccupations like urbanization or globalization, industrialization or education? China's leaders have faced the challenge of working out just how much they should stake on informatization, a process that few of them have really understood that well anyway.

Floridi and Sanders (2002) suggest a values-based approach is needed. They provide an overview of four possible approaches to characterizing the information society: the professional approach, which sees the field of information technology as something akin to medicine or law, and therefore demanding a set of professionally bounded information ethics; the radical approach, seeing the information age as transformative and novel – 'absolutely unique issues, in need of a unique approach'; the conservative approach – we only need a 'particular applied ethics, discussing new species of traditional moral issues'; and the innovative approach (one step down from the radical approach) that 'can expand the metaethical discourse with a substantially new perspective'. Floridi and Sanders conclude that the ethical issues raised by the information age 'are not uncontroversially unique' but 'are sufficiently novel to render inadequate the adoption of standard macroethics', such as utilitarianism. These authors argue for an information ethics in which the moral character of an action is evaluated according to its 'contribution to the growth of the infosphere' or, conversely, whether it 'negatively affects the whole infosphere'. They use the idea of 'infosphere' to enable an analysis about preservation and protection of the information society, by analogy with the idea of 'ecosphere' for the natural environment. In the philosophy of environmentalism, all parts of the ecosystem (living and non-living) have a potential moral value. These authors suggest that this approach is directly applicable to the infosphere: all information objects have a potential moral value. While this is a philosophical and ethical analysis, it does fly directly into policy. Floridi (2005) sees a direct practical application of his ethics: it 'provides the conceptual grounds that then guide problem-solving procedures'. He suggests that this approach 'deals with the descriptive analysis and critical evaluation of moral norms and values within as well as between information societies'. The implication of his approach is that while not everything changes fundamentally, everything in policy is affected sufficiently by the information society that it ought to be re-evaluated from that perspective. The infosphere is global and not nationally bounded. If a government does not have the policy values to promote the infosphere, to protect the information ecosystem of its corporations and citizens, then it will increasingly be out of step with the emergent global reality.

Floridi offers four dimensions for analysing the infosphere from a moral perspective, which can be slightly adapted to the policy domain as follows:

- acceptance of its political imperatives (assigning a social value to information and how it is used, as well as to the machines that produce and disseminate it)
- grasping the centrality of distributed political morality (pre-existing moral and political authority becomes disaggregated, and a reaggregated collective responsibility emerges)
- the enablers of hyper-information taking on a special political significance
- the welfare of information itself becoming a central reference point.

Taking a lead from this analysis, I have picked out a set of nine ideal policy values needed to foster the emergence and growth of an advanced information society that we can apply to the China case. They can be grouped into three sets as follows.

National information ecosystem

The first and perhaps dominating policy value that national leaders must observe on the domestic stage concerns the flourishing of information in the infosphere. There has to be freedom of information flow, freedom to aggregate it, and freedom to disseminate it. Even if this information reaggregation is seen as a purely economic activity, the associated political value is indistinguishable from freedom of conscience (the moral, political, scientific or artistic choices the person handling the information might make). A second value relates both to the social protection of that freedom and to the social incentives to make ever more creative and beneficial aggregations and reassessments of information. This is the question of equitable and protected access to the tools of information use and the sources of information. The body politic has to provide legal and political accountability for security of information and its agents. A third value for the national infosphere is ensuring the reliability and trustworthiness of the information itself and its reaggregations. This policy dimension ranges from simple security of the data and networks through to the reliability of the medium of dissemination (such as a newspaper, a government statement, a scientific journal or a work of art). Lack of trust in the information or the medium of its dissemination undermines its value as a contribution towards an advanced information society.

Innovative information economy

Within the national infosphere, the society (comprising the population, processes of social exchange, political culture and institutions) should give a very high priority in practice to the goal of economic and social transformation through information innovation. This is the essence of the original concept of the knowledge economy first identified by Machlup in 1962. This value can be summarized in the phrase 'transformation intent'. A second policy value is a commitment to putting in place systems that promote an innovation economy. The country should provide a solid material base, with the structures and economic foundations for cutting-edge research, application and diffusion of advanced science and technology. A third policy value is the ability to marshal human resources in critical mass in key sectors. The country should be able to provide a suitably large, geographically spread and socially diverse pool of creative innovators, entrepreneurs (investors), regulators, managers and technicians who can operate together normatively and effectively to advance the goal of an information society. Innovators need be able to count on strong material incentives for individual creativity.

Global information ecosystem

As already suggested, some analysts see the infosphere and the innovation system as global, and not bounded by national borders. The infosphere and innovation system are in fact inherently transnational phenomena because they are heavily dependent for maximum well-being on deep integration between the economies of advanced countries. So in fact, the values identified for what one may provisionally call the domestic infosphere (freedom of information exchange, protection of information exchange, and trusted information) and for the innovative information economy (transformation intent, innovation system, an innovator class) have very close connections with the global information ecosystem. A country wanting to maximize its gains from the global information society to build an information society at home must create the environment in its external relations that complements the values it needs to adopt on the domestic stage.

Thus the first policy value concerning the global infosphere is commitment to peaceful order in it. There must be a normative concept of strategic stability in cyberspace built around the principles of a flourishing cross-border information flow and exploitation. A second policy value that each country must observe is a commitment to eliminate strategic confrontations with key countries that might hinder the development of either a global information society or the national part of it (within the borders of the state). The third internationally focused policy value is a commitment to the principle of interdependent informatized security, where states of differing information capability (and political systems) work proactively to combine information resources and assets to address regional and global problems, such as climate change, resource shortages or humanitarian disasters. This last policy value includes a commitment to recognizing and ameliorating the digital divide between rich and poor countries.

Table 1.2 summarizes the nine ideal values that are used as the framework for analysis in the following chapters.

These nine values (three sets of three) are broadly in line, either explicitly or implicitly, with the key highlights of China's NIP 2006–20 (Central Committee and State Council 2006) and with the *Roadmap*

Table 1.2: Nine ideal values for an information society

National information ecosystem
- freedom of information exchange
- protection of information exchange
- trusted information

Innovative information economy
- transformation intent
- innovation system
- innovator class

Global information ecosystem
- strategic stability
- bridging military divides
- interdependent informatized security

to 2050 laid out by the CAS (Li Guojie 2011). They are also broadly in line with the policy values described in a number of Western academic studies on the information society and policy, such as Castells (2005), and they are compatible with the main qualitative indicators used by the WEF in composing the NRI. The top ten countries in the NRI have for the most part adopted these public values, Singapore being a case in point.

The values of a country's leaders are not static. They can begin to approach some ideal more closely, but can just as easily turn away from it. The analysis of the performance of China's leaders against the ideal values sees this variability as the norm. But the variability has a practical implication. The trajectory of the variation from the ideal will determine the trajectory of the outcome. The more China's leaders depart from key values that underpin an information society, the less likely it is that an information society can emerge as powerfully as it might. The converse is also true.

That may be more or less self-evident, but there is one simple idea that has emerged from the study of international ethics that provides a scholarly foundation for making that judgement, while at the same time offering an important refinement on it. Frost (1986, 2009) has suggested that in ethical debates (a political contest of values) the outcome can be predicted by looking at the trajectory of the negotiations. In conversation with me, Frost has suggested that the information age has forced on China's leaders a need to negotiate their power and their values with new constituencies that they did not have to deal with at the height of the dictatorship. For Frost, the turning point or the opening point of this negotiation was the reluctant acceptance by the CCP leaders that the country could not modernize or achieve an information society without engaging powerful external forces in the provision of essential technical expertise or investment, and powerful internal constituencies that were not committed to doctrinaire Communism.

Frost has argued that while there are underlying norms (values) in the system of states, neither the states nor the norms have a privileged position. Norms adjust as new circumstances arise. In what Frost calls the 'difficult cases' (using the example of justifications for terrorism), the process of change – if it is to occur – is one of negotiation between 'individuals', either as persons or as representatives of larger groups, such as states, civil society, multinational corporations, or international interest-based organizations. This approach suggests that neither the norms nor the institutions (the outcomes) are predetermined. Progressive change cannot be automatically assumed. Frost has not addressed the predictive power of his theory in any detail, but one value of it may be that for a given set of 'negotiators', the outcome in terms of consensus around a norm might reasonably be predicted from the trajectory of the negotiations.

Thus, drawing on Frost, we can conclude that the decision by the leaders that China should become an information society through heavy reliance on foreign sources has an immediate ethical dimension, and an inevitably dialogic character, regardless of the preferences of the leaders to avoid or deny such a dialogue. It is both intergovernmental and non-governmental (the latter through massively increased personal and private sector communications and exchange across the borders). Because of the non-governmental aspect, the Chinese leaders have also put themselves reluctantly into new moral dialogue about values with domestic constituencies.

The following chapter reviews the development of informatization in China up to the end of 1999 to establish the policy values that were in place as its leaders embarked on their plan to position the country competitively in the global information revolution. It has been a journey of politics and society broadly defined, of economics and technological development, and of international cooperation and confrontation. But underneath all of that, it has been a contest between the CCP leaders and others about the ethical choices involved.

2 | Legacy Values

China's leaders at the highest level publicly embraced the information society ambition for the first time in 2000. This chapter revisits the lurching evolution of repression and reform policies that brought leadership values affecting the information society to where they were at that stepping-off point. The purpose in offering a very brief historical perspective is not to provide a potted survey of events that are treated more articulately, at great length and in compelling detail elsewhere. The intent here is to review those events through the lens of the ideal policy values for the information society referred to in chapter 1. What were the legacy settings in place by the year 2000 as the leaders tried to reach more decisively for an information society? The importance of an historical perspective for understanding China's outcomes in informatization has been highlighted by research on national innovation systems. Farina and Preissl (2000) point out that innovation is by nature a social process that involves people and institutions. It is also by nature 'dynamic and open to external interaction'. As this chapter shows in the case of China, a national innovation system is 'path-dependent' (though not linear) and is always the result of the 'local socio-economic history'. The chapter follows a chronological treatment, concluding with a summary assessment of leadership values in 1999 compared with the ideal values.

WAR AGAINST INFORMATION AND SOCIETY

From 1949 to 1966, the CCP became progressively more dictatorial in its suppression of the primary values of an information society: the free exchange of ideas and data, promotion of unfettered economic and social innovation, and pursuit of peaceful international policies that would help achieve it. The war against information exchange and creativity permeated the entire fabric of society down to the most personal level. The leaders justified these policies as necessary while the material foundations of the new China were being built. But these material foundations did depend on science, and less than a month after the new Communist government was declared, the CAS was created. Thus there have consistently been two channels of information flow in China that have dominated leadership views: the Communist Party's propaganda and control channel (under which culture was subsumed) and the scientific development channel.

This was particularly evident in the launch by the country's leader Mao Zedong of a campaign in 1956 for critical evaluation of the government: the 'policy of letting a hundred flowers bloom and a hundred schools of thought contend is designed to promote the flourishing of the arts and the progress of science', Mao said. The campaign was suppressed almost as soon as it had been put in place and those who spoke out, many from within the CCP, were jailed or persecuted. The sorry fate of the 'hundred flowers campaign' was a salutary lesson for anyone in the country seeking to pursue information openness and independent analysis.

The reliance on ideology over scientific information was strongly in evidence in 1958 when Mao launched a radical experiment in economic development called the Great Leap Forward, which was accompanied by a devastating three-year famine causing the premature death of tens of millions of people. Mao's number two and eventual successor as leader, Deng Xiaoping, later lamented that he had not offered any sort of scientific analysis and information to speak out against the Great Leap policy (Vogel 2011). Yet it was also in 1958 that China built its first computer, based on designs and a machine obtained from the USSR.

Between 1958 and 1962, China progressively broke off its relations with the USSR, its main source of advanced scientific information and technology. In 1964, China exploded its first nuclear device, an achievement that was a small miracle given the poor developmental state of the country. This breakthrough was in large part achieved through the involvement of scientists of Chinese origin returning from the United States and through training programmes for Chinese scientists in the USSR between 1950 and 1960.

By 1965, China's economy was dominated by rural livelihoods (completely contained in non-voluntary collective farms, which owned all rural land) and by heavy industry (all in state-owned factories to which employees were assigned on a non-voluntary basis). Illiteracy – an obstacle of the most fundamental kind to an information society – was a defining characteristic of many parts of the country. China had a centrally planned, command economy. Private ownership of business, of homes and of land was illegal. Entrepreneurship was regarded as morally bankrupt. The education system in schools and universities was highly structured, highly ideological and not supportive of creativity and innovation except for trumpeting the superiority of the Communist system and shoring up CCP rule. In the majority of households, a light bulb was the only electric instrument of any kind. (That year China set up its Household Electric Appliance Research Institute.) Imports of foreign goods were highly controlled and mostly comprised commodities and heavy machinery. China's prison camps for political detainees were at least on the same scale as those in the USSR – but probably much more numerous. China's society was highly militarized and the country cut off from most of the world. It was engaged in a military confrontation with the USSR, it had fought a short border war with India in 1962, and it had disputes over most of its other land borders. It saw the United States as its ideological and military adversary because of the US alliance with the Republic of China (ROC) on Taiwan and because China was militantly anti-capitalist.

Worse was to come in 1966 in the form of a new ideological campaign launched by Mao: the Great Proletarian Cultural Revolution. This has been the single most important historical experience after 1949 in terms of defining the policy settings and modes of decision-making for China's information society as they were at the turn of this century. Explanations differ as to the precise causes of the Cultural Revolution, but it was in all practical terms a political struggle between an extremist view of what revolutionary China should be and a more measured, pragmatic, though still Communist and totalitarian view. During the first two years of the Cultural Revolution, the intellectual class in China (the very foundation of an innovative information society) had been branded as 'stinking weeds' and systematically repressed through country-wide violence at the hands of organized Red Guard units. In some cases, this included summary executions. By 1967, most universities had ceased functioning, and millions of intellectuals lucky enough to be spared a worse fate were sent to rural areas for re-education – usually to work as farm labourers.

The death toll from 'revolution actions' by Red Guards probably ran into hundreds of thousands, according to statistics from just two provinces provided by Yang Su (2011). In 1967, Mao ordered the suppression of the Red Guards movement and a restoration of civil order. The persecution of scientists and scientific workers continued after the mass violence ended. The number of scientific journals in print fell from 400 in 1965 to 20 in 1969 (Brock 2009). International interchange for scientific development was almost non-existent.

China's policies remained highly confrontational, deeply ideological and totalitarian for a number of years. They were not conducive to the development of science and technology even though the strident nationalism of the CCP demanded evidence of scientific progress as proof of the inherent superiority of its ideology. This latter impulse helped protect key programmes through the Cultural Revolution period. For example, in 1967, at the height of the political turmoil across the country, China was able to marshal enough expertise to explode its first hydrogen bomb. The leaders were also protecting computer technology research in the CAS and in 1968 China produced the first integrated circuit (microchip) made in the country. (Integrated circuits are the basic components of most electronic products.) In spite of these niche technological successes in China, there was for the most part little freedom and creativity in the sciences. Intervention (supervision) from non-specialist Communist Party officials was embedded in the fabric of all scientific work units.

In 1969, China was forced to moderate its armed border provocations against the USSR because the latter threatened war, including possible nuclear attack, if it did not. China sought international allies urgently and turned to the United States, which had sensed the opportunity well. This period was the start of the end of China's international isolation. In domestic policy, science and education were early beneficiaries of an easing of extremism. In 1970, Tsinghua University recommenced enrolment in small numbers, one of only a handful of universities to do so (Anon. 1972).

US president Richard Nixon visited China in 1972 and the People's Republic of China (PRC) took the China seat in the UN, displacing the ROC (on Taiwan). The events heralded the opening up of China to relatively limited exchanges with the developed world that would prove to be essential for China's recovery from the scientific and technical stagnation it had imposed on itself. Yet a group of American computer specialists who visited China in 1972 concluded that the country 'is officially committed to a course of progress which does not permit the establishment of a scientific/technical elite' (Anon. 1972). This was a period of anti-science in China, when, as part of its Cultural Revolution, the highest value in science was 'redness' or quality of communistic ideological purity. Expertise was regarded as a lesser, almost counter-revolutionary value.

It took the death of Mao in 1976 before any reversal of the ideological crusade, including its anti-science and anti-information elements, could begin. His eventual successor after a brief interregnum was Deng Xiaoping, who later referred to the Cultural Revolution as a 'full scale civil war', noting that it had 'wasted the talents of a whole generation of our people', and that the effects 'didn't stop with just one generation' (Deng 1980). A later CCP general secretary, Jiang Zemin, described its influence on the country's technology sector as a 'catastrophe' (Jiang 2010). One notable victim of the persecution apart from Deng had been Xi Zhongxun, a revolutionary leader and the father of the CCP general secretary as of 2012, Xi Jinping. Like many other party leaders, Xi the elder had been subject to persecution, jail or other forms of confinement from 1968 to 1975, when the younger Xi was between 15 and 23 years old. Thus, this period was a hugely formative influence on the current generation of Chinese leaders when they were in their late teens and early twenties.

REFORM AND OPENING UP: TECHNOLOGY PLEASE

The new CCP leaders who took power within two years of the death of Mao realized that the CCP had brought the country to economic bankruptcy and a developmental impasse that were self-inflicted. Political persecutions of intellectuals and citizens were scaled back, universities reopened, and international scientific exchanges gathered pace. The leaders launched a policy called the 'four modernizations': in agriculture, industry, science and technology, and national defence. This policy, sponsored by Deng Xiaoping, and building on an earlier effort dating back as far as 1963, was announced in December 1978. Although the four modernizations policy foreshadowed some use of foreign technologies and expertise, its essential vision was one of self-reliance or autarky. The policy represented the belief that China could by and large marshal its own resources, and, with just a little help from outsiders, emerge as a powerful country in later generations. The use of foreign technologies had been branded by the leaders of the Cultural Revolution as politically unacceptable. In 1978, China signed its first contracts with leading American firms, such as Boeing (for the supply of modern civil aircraft), and signed a peace treaty with Japan that was a harbinger of large development loans, scientific exchange and some technology transfer from Japan.

The first cracks in China's totalitarian public values around information policy began to appear in 1978. Deng planted the seeds of reform on a wide front, in both domestic and international policy. But all were experiments rather than wholesale commitments. Three of these experiments in particular were to be more significant than others. The first was a decision in April 1979 to set up a special economic zone in Shenzhen (in Guangdong province adjacent to Hong Kong) and three others in locations on the coast. They were to be enclaves of foreign-invested factories that could be isolated legally and socially from the rest of China. (This reform was led in Guangdong by the first secretary of the province, the aforementioned Xi Zhongxun. So his son, the CCP general secretary Xi Jinping, was intimately familiar with the politics of the reform era at the absolute outset in a way that no other current leader has been.) The second was the trial of a new system of economic control in agriculture called the Household Responsibility System, which allowed farmers, all in state-owned collective farms called communes, to sell produce that exceeded state quotas and keep the money for their own household. The purpose was to incentivize higher farm labour productivity. The third experiment, to be very short-lived, was the call for 'big democracy'.

On this last question, 'big democracy', stirrings of interest in a liberalization of the Chinese system by reference to Western standards of human rights burst onto the public stage in 1978. In December, as part of an embryonic round of public protest against the legacy of Mao Zedong, a political activist in China, Wei Jingsheng, described democratization as the country's 'fifth modernization', to play off the official formula of the four modernizations (Wei 1978). In his short manifesto posted on Democracy Wall, Wei cited Albert Einstein: 'Everything that is really great and inspiring is created by the individual who can labour in freedom.'

The authorities suppressed these activities after a relatively short period and Wei was imprisoned for fifteen years. In a speech to the Central Committee on 30 March 1979, Deng Xiaoping provided the ideological orthodoxy to justify continued suppression of the free flow of ideas going forward (Deng 1979). It was the doctrine of four cardinal principles or the 'four upholds':

- adhere to the socialist road ('based on public ownership')
- uphold the dictatorship of the proletariat
- uphold the leadership of the Communist Party
- uphold Marxism-Leninism and Mao Zedong Thought.

While setting severe limits on freedom of exchange of ideas and information, the speech by Deng also gave a positive signal for further technological development. He emphasized that self-reliance supplemented by foreign aid and the acquisition of advanced technology from abroad had always been Communist China's path. He maintained a firm intention to quarantine technological imports from any contamination with Western political ideas. He foreshadowed a 'vast increase' in normal contacts with foreigners for scientific exchange and for investment (even though China had no laws permitting such investment at the time). Deng recognized the link between a pragmatically creative ideology based on education and the rule of law: 'We have neglected the study of political science, law, sociology and world politics, and now we must hurry to make up our deficiencies in these subjects.' He admitted that China did not have the basic 'information' about its own country that it needed for effective policy: 'for years we haven't even had adequate statistical data in the social sciences.'

In international affairs, Deng visited the United States in January 1979 to mark the formal establishment of diplomatic relations and to promote technology transfer to China. He also used the visit to discuss with US president Jimmy Carter China's imminent invasion of Vietnam. Its purpose was to teach Vietnam a lesson for invading China's political ally, Cambodia; for allying itself militarily with the USSR; and for the expulsion of some ethnic Chinese. Though the invasion was short-lived and limited in scope, China kept up military and geopolitical pressure on Vietnam for a decade. This military action showed that, for China, the big decisions on reform, which depended in part on peaceful international relations, were not ever going to be big enough to alter its strategic calculations of when to use military force to defend key geopolitical interests.

Even though China had launched its 'opening up' policy in 1978, it moved slowly at first on what information was allowed in. By 1983, the floodgates had begun to open. While there were still many banned publications, a number of ideologically acceptable or politically neutral foreign publications began to be printed by local publishers. The bestselling foreign book in China in 1983 was Alvin Toffler's *The Third Wave* (1980), which canvassed the transformation of the global political economy and human society under the influence of information technology, access to space, and a number of other transformative technologies. Both Deng and the premier, Zhao Ziyang, are reputed to have studied the Toffler book. Its arguments that the Chinese leaders found persuasive related to the revolutionary role of new information technologies in determining power relationships in the world. Toffler argued that the countries most likely to lead the world in power terms would be those that mastered the new technologies. The Toffler book's influence at that time was so profound that two decades later the *People's Daily* (03/08/2006), China's leading official newspaper, named Toffler among the fifty most influential foreigners in modern Chinese history.

This was the environment in which the leaders decided in 1983 to give the electronics industry a much higher priority and committed to increasing its output eight-fold by the year 2000 (Jiang 2010). They were setting goals for this industry to outperform the rest of the economy by at least 100 per cent. It was in January 1983 that *Time Magazine* named the personal computer 'Machine of the Year' (instead of naming a person of the year), with Apple producing its first highly popular model (the IIe) in the United States and elsewhere; Microsoft Windows was first released; and software for intranets became commercially available. At the time, personal computers, already available in Hong Kong and Taiwan in early models as consumer items for the household and office, were very rare in mainland China and certainly not available anywhere in the country for legal private purchase.

When China sought in 1983 to embark on its first information revolution (which it saw at the time as limited largely to the technology and the machines), it was in the grip of a sharp political power struggle between reformers and conservatives. In 1983, Toffler's book had been branded by the conservatives as 'spiritual pollution' as part of their campaign against the reformers and against most things foreign. The flood into China of Western ideas, people and books was shaking China's political system, and major planks of Communist ideology, to the core.

Deng was determined to shake China up. In 1984, some Chinese companies were allowed to issue shares for private ownership, a practice previously seen as anathema to Communism. Deng spoke at the inauguration of the newspaper *Economic Information Daily*, emphasizing the link between new information resources and the four modernizations, and on another occasion he was reported to have said that every child in China should learn computer skills (Qu 2010). On the political stage, he called for the convening of a Special Conference of the CCP, at an unspecified date but two to three years ahead of the scheduled changeover date, to engineer a large number of retirements from the Politburo and Central Committee in favour of the appointment of younger and more liberal people.

The constitutional coup by Deng with the Special Conference, held in 1985, ushered in an even more stormy debate about the country's values. Economic reforms were broadly accepted as necessary, but there was great consternation in the Party over the political significance of the measures. Radical political reform premised on non-Communist values was emerging as a possible vector for China. One of the key campaign themes of the conservatives was the idea that China was being subjected to 'spiritual pollution' from the West that was contrary to the ethical foundations of Communism.

They were right. Private entrepreneurship in Chinese-owned industry was making its first comeback. In 1986, the CAS invested RMB200,000 (around US$25,000 at the time) to fund eleven people in a start-up called the New Technology Developer Inc. This was the forerunner of the Legend Group, which subsequently became Lenovo (now the world's biggest producer of personal computers). In 1987, the first connection by a Chinese institution to the internet occurred. The Institute of Computer Application in Beijing set up the China Academic Network (CANET), operating only for email, and routed through Karlsruhe in Germany (Chen and Chu 1995).

INFORMATION ECONOMY WITHOUT FREEDOM
OF INFORMATION

In 1987, the concept of an open information economy was adopted by CCP leaders trying to reform China's application of Marxism and the command economy. For those opposed to a more open information flow, the priority was about retaining dictatorship and thought control, opposing Western influences and ending the political careers of the more liberal Party members. This was a struggle between advocates of information and advocates of ideology. By 1987, the political struggle began to turn in favour of the orthodox ideologues. The more liberal CCP general secretary Hu Yaobang, appointed to the top leadership only in 1981, was forced to step down because of his alleged mishandling of student demonstrations that began in late 1986. Understanding the deep divisions within the leadership, students in the universities were beginning to revolt. The same year, the vice-president of the China University of Science and Technology (CUST), Fang Lizhi, a well-known physicist, was dismissed from his post and expelled from the Communist Party. Early in 1989 he published an article severely critical of the Chinese government: 'socialism of the Lenin-Stalin-Mao variety has been quite thoroughly discredited' (Fang 1989). He referred to the May Fourth Movement of 1919 in China, in which the issue of modern technology had been an issue. He said that the 'slogan "science and democracy" is once again circulating, and becoming a new source for hope among Chinese intellectuals'. Fang made a blistering attack on the anti-science policies of the CCP. He explained that 'Ignorance serves dictatorship well. The true reason for the destruction of education is apparent enough.'

The intensity of this contest and the severity of its effect in China at the time can be quickly gauged from the signature events in the most iconic political locations in the country in a two-month period from 15 April to 4 June 1989. On 21 April, the eve of the official funeral for deposed general secretary Hu, large overnight student demonstrations triggered similar demonstrations and sit-ins in the following six weeks throughout China, with calls for humanism, Western-style democracy and an end to official corruption. Workers joined the protest actions. Tiananmen Square in the centre of Beijing, adjacent to the leadership compound of Zhongnanhai, was occupied by demonstrators for over a month. During a meeting in the Great Hall of the People (on one side of Tiananmen Square) that the leaders hoped would force a back-down by the protesters, one of the student leaders, dressed in pyjamas, berated and humiliated Chinese premier Li Peng in scenes that were captured on national television – an event the likes of which had not been seen since the Cultural Revolution. On 20 May, the government declared martial law, mobilizing around 250,000 troops to enter the capital. On the evening of 3 June, Deng and Li ordered troops to clear Tiananmen Square. This started a military and police repression of the democracy movement across the country, killing hundreds of unarmed people and arresting thousands. Hundreds of students and other pro-testers managed to flee from China. Western countries imposed a deep freeze on relations with it and foreign investment in the country dropped sharply. The general secretary of just two years standing, Zhao Ziyang, was demoted and put under house arrest. His purge was espe-cially significant because he was the second leader of the CCP forced to step down in two years. He remained under house arrest until his death in 2005, but succeeded in breaking the information ban imposed on him by recording a memoir to audio cassette tapes that led to its publication in the West in 2009 (Zhao Ziyang 2009). Zhao's former secretary, who accompanied him to Tiananmen Square in a famous last effort to convince the protesters to leave it, was Wen Jiabao, who subsequently became premier of China from 2003 to 2013, and who was later one of the leading advocates of informatization in the leadership.

The events were so momentous that Chinese leaders were obliged to propagandize their view both of the demonstrations and of the issues they had raised. The leadership views were firmly imposed on the public consciousness of the country, including through trials of some of the demonstrators and a massive propaganda campaign. The task was made easier by the Communist Party's control of mass media, particularly television. The main lines dictated from the top were (a) stability is everything; (b) public protest intended to bring about political reform will not be tolerated; and (c) the Communist Party leadership will bear almost any cost internationally and domestically to ensure the survival not just of the Party but of its specific leaders at any time.

The replacement for Zhao as CCP general secretary was Jiang Zemin, the former minister of the Ministry of Electronics Industry (MEI), who in 1983 had loyally followed Deng down the path of making that sector grow twice as fast as the rest of the economy. At the time, Jiang was a Politburo member and Party secretary in Shanghai. The accession of Jiang to the top CCP post ensured that informatization had a champion at the highest level of Chinese politics from 1989 until 2005. But Jiang was chosen because of respect in the leadership for his smooth suppression of dissent in Shanghai, a course of action that was the very antithesis of an open information society.

Once again, as in the 1958 suppression of the 'hundred flowers' campaign, the CCP had made the intellectuals and freedom of information (FOI) the enemies of the state. The suppression was propagandized around the country as the highest virtue. This led to an exodus abroad of some of the country's best talents and most spirited reformers. Hundreds had fled in the immediate aftermath of the use of force in Tiananmen Square, but tens of thousands followed in the decade afterwards, largely by taking up scholarships for foreign study. Fang Lizhi, former vice-president of the country's leading S&T university, who had sought asylum in the US embassy on 6 June 1989, was finally allowed to leave the embassy and China one full year later to travel to self-imposed exile in the United States.

The lesson for all Chinese from these momentous events, as from the earlier victimization of intellectuals, was that over forty years, the Communist Party was, at a high moral level, both anti-science and anti-information. The lesson for Chinese leaders at all levels in politics and science was that their personal liberty was at risk if they advocated a 'science before the Party' approach.

Not everything in these few years was retrenchment. For example, in 1989, the leaders approved the creation of the China Electronics Corporation, as a state-owned spin-off from the MEI. It would later become the biggest Chinese electronics company, including in the area of military informatization and state security. In 1990, Legend launched its first original PC in China, transforming itself from importer to manufacturer. That year, the CUST got approval to initiate a PhD programme in computer software. And as a clear indicator of the return of capitalism, the Shenzhen Stock Exchange was set up and the Shanghai Stock Exchange reopened, having been closed since the CCP came to power in 1949. In 1991, China made the extraordinary decision to allow Taiwan to join the recently formed APEC group. Taiwan was already an important source of investment for China. The argument was made that since this was an economic grouping, and not formally an international organization, Taiwan could be admitted as an 'economy'. Also in 1991, the Institute of High Energy Physics (IHEP) was the first organization in China to lease a direct international line on the internet that connected it to the Linear Accelerator Center at Stanford University in the United States.

CONSOLIDATING THE INFORMATION ECONOMY

As profoundly negative for the future of the information society ambition as the political turning points of 1989 were, the subsequent decade revealed a space for innovation, liberalization and pluralism that would have defied the imagination or expectations of most observers in the immediate aftermath of the events of that year. The turn was evident in 1992 with the rehabilitation of Hu Qili, one of the most important party leaders demoted in the 1989 purge. He was appointed to the post of deputy minister of the MEI and a year later to minister, the post that Jiang Zemin had himself occupied a decade earlier. The leaders were making an unmistakable recommitment to the need for talented, energetic leaders who understood the political implications of informatization and reform.

The associated government-wide decision that year was the elevation of the information economy to the status of 'important objective'. A National Informatization Joint Conference (NIJC) was set up to lead the effort. The CCP appeared to be moving quickly with the related decision one year later to set up a new corporation, China Unicom, to manage mobile phones independently of China Telecom, the state-owned body. Also in 1994, China established a National Informatization Expert Team and took the first steps towards accessing the internet. The Sino–US Joint Committee on Science and Technology and the American National Science Foundation agreed that the National Computing and Networking Facility of China and the CAS could link to the internet. On the legal side, China introduced its Regulation on Security and Protection of Computer Information Systems and made corresponding changes to its criminal law. Jiang Zemin met Microsoft founder Bill Gates, though this first meeting was not a happy one because of Jiang's irritation with Gates' insistence on free market economics and because Microsoft had developed a new Chinese version of Windows in Taiwan.

The technical and infrastructure advances continued apace. On 1 January 1995, China Telecom made the first public internet connection to the United States through the American telephone company Sprint. Its bandwidth was significantly lower than that made between Taiwan and the United States in August the same year (64k compared with the 1,544k link). In March, the CAS linked its branches in Shanghai, Hefei, Wuhan and Nanjing through the internet, thus making the first effort to extend internet coverage outside Beijing and Shanghai. In May, China Telecom started work on a national backbone network for Chinanet. In August, the Shuimu Qinghua bulletin board system (bbs) built in the China Education and Research Network (CERNET) went into operation. It was the first internet-based bbs (electronic bulletin board system) in the mainland. In terms of domestic research in information technology, the CUST set up the country's first National High Performance Computing Center. Bill Gates visited Jiang Zemin in China a second time. Gates' visit was a clear portent of the leaders' determination to co-opt the most advanced IT corporations from the West in their pursuit of informatization. This commitment was further demonstrated by leaders' acceptance of the opening in China in 1995 of an office to lobby for the protection of the collective interests of major US information technology corporations operating there. This office, operating formally as a non-profit under the rubric of the United States Information Technology Office, became a powerful force for harmonizing China's industrial policies with what might loosely be called international best practice (as seen from the IT corporate perspective).

The same year, China engineered another dramatic chilling in its relations with key foreign partners in its information economy ambition when it sought to influence the evolution of politics in Taiwan through military pressure, conducting what it said were test launches of its medium-range ballistic missiles to splash down in sea areas adjacent to Taiwan. The tests were repeated in March 2006. China was reacting to a series of statements by Taiwan's president, Li Teng-hui, about the island's political status and associated US statements and decisions.

In 1996, a major breakthrough in informatization policy was imminent. That year, the leaders decided to upgrade the pre-existing joint conference for national informatization (the NIJC) and set up the SILG within the State Council. The head of the new SILG was a vice-premier, as with the NIJC, but the new group was to meet once or twice per month instead of twice per year as before. In the same year, China also set up a Working Group on Information Security that reported to the SILG (Qu 2010). Also in 1996, China had its eye on stepping up aspects of its military informatization. Communist Party general secretary Jiang Zemin told a military audience that 'seizing information dominance' would become a 'focus in warfare' (Jiang 2010).

In February 1997, Deng Xiaoping died, without any immediately visible effect on policy since he had been almost fully retired for five years. But his dualistic political legacy on opening and reform, while containing threats to the information dictatorship around Party rule, was intact.

The structural reforms around the information economy began to bear fruit in 1997, with the first National Conference on Informatization approving plans for informatization of the country. (This conference was more broadly based than the similarly named NIJC.) The conference was held in Shenzhen and took a fateful decision not to follow a Western pathway to informatization but to follow a distinctly Chinese path by emphasizing the link between informatization and the more traditional Chinese priority of industrialization (Qu 2010). In contrast, the more liberal-minded Hu Qili took the view that 'infor-matisation takes the lead on China's industrialisation' (Duan 2012). The distinction was important. By linking informatization and indus-trialization as a pair, the leaders were providing a way for the more conservative forces to hold back the claims of the informatization champions and maintain a measured pace of industrialization that most leaders saw as quite distinct from, rather than depending on, informatization.

The 1997 conference was something of a late arrival. It was con-vened to approve a plan that had been developed in 1995 under the title 'National Informatization Development Plan', which reportedly set out very general objectives for 2010. The document declared the internet to be a part of the state information infrastructure and pro-posed the establishment of a State Internet Information Center and Internet Exchange Center. The body to emerge in 1997 was the China

Internet Network Information Center (CNNIC), located within the CAS, to be the 'builder, operator and administrator of the infrastructure for China's information society' (www1.cnnic.cn). The conference called on the government to ascribe to the electronic information industry the status of 'pillar of the national economy'; for the creation of a talent pool of IT professionals specializing in research, development, production and applications; and for the popularizing of IT awareness and education. This was not a comprehensive plan for the informatization of the economy but rather a plan to bring the information technology industry to the forefront of economic planning for the first time.

That year, China tightened its security grip on the internet by setting up a Public Information Network Security Monitoring Bureau. The criminal law was further tightened to cover use of the internet for fraud, theft, graft, embezzlement and theft of state secrets, among other acts (Qu 2010). One of the earliest advances in informatization for social welfare came when Hewlett Packard helped the People's Liberation Army (PLA) develop the country's most advanced Health Information System, later adopted in major hospitals.

In the world of politics, two historic events with significant implications for China's information economy occurred in 1997. The first was the resumption of Chinese sovereignty over Hong Kong. It showed, or would come to show, that the country that had so ruthlessly imposed an information dictatorship was now prepared to tolerate or live with information pluralism of a kind, under the formula 'one country, two systems', devised by Deng fifteen years earlier to seal negotiations with the UK on the return of Hong Kong to Chinese sovereignty. The higher political import of the formula was that it would also apply in the future to Taiwan, if it would agree to peaceful reunification with China. When China resumed sovereignty of Hong Kong in 1997, it was a momentous event in its own right, but for China's leaders it also held out some promise of a similar resumption of sovereignty over

Taiwan. The second historic event was the alteration of the CCP constitution to allow business people to join the party. The CCP had become the place to do business, and it was around the mid-1990s that leading political figures came to be identified more by the general public with significant business interests, including by corrupt means.

The CAS set up its own leading group on informatization in 1997, well ahead of other sub-national entities. The CCP leaders commissioned a report from the CAS on 'The Coming of the Knowledge-Based Economy and Construction of a National Innovation System', which was completed that year. This report prompted action by the government in the areas of R&D, intellectual property rights (IPR) and venture capital (Suttmeier and Shi 2008). The turnkey role of the United States in China's informatization came into further relief with the launch in 1997 of the first web portal, itc.com.cn (later to become sohu.com), by a Chinese-owned company, albeit one incorporated in Delaware in the United States.

The whirlwind of reform in favour of informatization was about to gain in intensity. In March 1998, the new premier, Zhu Rongji, came to office and unleashed massive structural reforms in the economy. There were four planks to the radical shake-up: strong economic leadership to sweep away the last vestiges of doctrinaire socialism; radical reform of the armed forces and defence industry; strong legal leadership to build durable foundations for a stable market society; and the expansion of democracy. China had a new set of public values: to become rich, strong, democratic and civilized (Austin 2001). Notably, the government set up a new Ministry of Information Industry (MII). This was a turning point in leadership attitudes to the information economy. It saw the merging of two ministries (Electronics Industry and Posts and Telecommunications) and other agencies (including notably elements of the China Aviation Industry Corporation and the China Aerospace Industry Corporation). The MII also took over the role of the pre-existing SILG office, which had served as the interdepartmental coordinating body for informatization policy. The MII was established to promote reform of the telecoms sector, to bring about the separation of the functions of government and enterprises, to separate management of post offices and telecom offices, to restructure telecom systems and to reform the associated SOEs, such as China Telecom.

The security agencies were tracking with the reforms. In 1998, the Ministry of Public Security (MPS) launched a pilot for the Golden Shield project, to begin to work towards setting up a capability for monitoring all computer networks in China for a variety of purposes (political control, crime prevention, public order and protecting social morality).

That year, Microsoft set up the first foreign-invested ICT research lab in China, called Microsoft Research China (renamed in 2001 as Microsoft Research Asia). It was later to become the company's largest basic research institution outside the United States. Intel opened its China Research Centre that year too. The China Patent Office was renamed the State Intellectual Property Office (SIPO), a government agency directly under the leadership of the State Council. The first of twelve annual white papers on IPR in China was published. The 1997 CAS report on the knowledge economy led to the Knowledge Innovation Programme (KIP), to be piloted by the CAS beginning in 1998; five of its nineteen programmes set in motion between 1999 and 2001 involved ICT-related sciences, and the other fourteen would not have been possible without advanced computing (Suttmeier and Shi 2008). A related measure, one year later, was the decision to force the country's research institutes to become self-supporting by relying much more on market forces.

The constellation of private sector interests that would come to define much of China's information society began to shine more brightly in 1999 when Sina.com, an internet services company, was established through the merger of a Chinese company and the

US-based Sunnyvale (operating the largest Chinese-language news site in the world for Chinese speakers in the United States, Taiwan, Singapore and elsewhere). In that year, Sina quickly overtook Sohu as the platform of choice, a trajectory and position that it has maintained since. In Chinese, the name of Sina is *xinlang*, which means 'new wave'. It was also in 1999 that two Chinese entrepreneurs returning to China from the United States set up EachNet, an eBay equivalent; and OICQ (an instant messaging service modelled on an AOL service called ICQ and MSN Messenger) was set up. Table 2.1 shows a short list of internet start-ups to 1999.

Internal security remained a primary focus of leadership attention. In 1999, the year that the Yahoo! search engine became accessible in China, the MII and the MPS jointly set up a network security management centre to devise rules for electronic technology, information transmission and reception. The Hong Kong office of these two

Table 2.1: Start-up dates for public Chinese internet platforms, 1997–1999

BRAND NAME ON LAUNCH (BRAND NAME NOW)	PLATFORM TYPE	YEAR
Itc.com.cn (Sohu)	Web portal	1997
Netease (163.com)	Email and web hosting	1997
Sina.com	Web portal	1999
Alibaba	Business-to-business global sales	1999
EachNet (bought by eBay in 2013)	Person-to-person sales	1999
eLong	Travel information	1999
cTrip.com	Travel information	1999
OICQ (Ten Cent QQ)	Short message service	1999

agencies, along with the local branch of China's Ministry of State Security (MSS), actually issued a call for all state and private organizations not to connect their systems to the internet. MII acted on fears that imported computers and software would be affected by Trojans or backdoors, and called for the development of domestically made computers and software systems to be increased. In both Taiwan and China, patriotic hackers were regularly penetrating the other side's computer systems.

The increasing openness of China to the information society in the last years of the decade received a serious setback in July 1999 when a nationwide group, Falun Dafa or Falun Gong, with followers estimated in the tens of millions, staged a demonstration of around 10,000 people outside the leadership compound in Zhongnanhai in Beijing. The movement was not political in intent, but rather an outgrowth of a resurgence of nationwide interest in China's history and culture, particularly various traditions of *qi gong*. Within days of the surprise demonstration on the northwestern corner of Tiananmen Square, the country's internal security apparatus was mobilized against it and the organization was banned. The Party leadership's overreaction to the Falun Gong movement can perhaps be attributed in large part to an overestimation of that movement's informational potential. This may have been fuelled by rumours and statements from the Falun Gong leader that the internet had played a central role in getting out the 10,000 demonstrators. But by the next year, the movement was streaming its radio live over the internet to make it available in China (Bell and Boas 2003). The leaders' suppression of information about Falun Gong and membership of it was subsequently felt throughout China – in schools, universities, the CCP and the armed forces. Members were persecuted, jailed and on occasion tortured.

China's leaders began to pay a lot more attention to information warfare (IW) in 1999 after the United States bombed the intelligence and communications wing of the Chinese embassy in Belgrade in the NATO campaign against the Former Yugoslavia. Jiang briefed the CMC on the critical role played by high technology in that campaign (Jiang 2010). It was later revealed that Chinese communications staff in the Chinese embassy were rebroadcasting command and control information for the defending Serbian forces. It was also only later that reports began appearing that the United States had successfully used advanced cyber warfare techniques, including electronic warfare techniques, to manipulate power and telephone grids in Belgrade. According to one source, the PLA set up the first cyber warfare units in its headquarters in 1999 (Hwang 2012), though they had existed earlier in lower-level units. The precise purpose of these units (in terms of what sort of IW activities they engaged in) has not been revealed. An authoritative 1999 assessment of China's military cyber capabilities concluded that 'the available evidence suggests that the PLA does not currently have a coherent IW doctrine, certainly nothing compared to U.S. doctrinal writings on the subject' (Mulvenon 1999). The capabilities 'do not match even the primitive sophistication of their underlying strategies, which call for stealth weapons, joint operations, battlefield transparency, long-range precision strike, and real-time intelligence.'

SUMMARY ASSESSMENT OF LEADERSHIP VALUES IN 1999

By the end of 1999, the information society as an idea was clearly in play in China but the leaders had not committed to it. They had as yet only articulated the goal of becoming a knowledge economy or an information economy. As a result, all of the ideal values for achieving the broader vision of an information society were not particularly prominent. Here is a summary evaluation of the mismatch in 1999 between the actual values of China's leadership and each of the ideal values needed for an information society, as listed in table 1.2.

National information ecosystem

Freedom of information exchange: The leaders were, at that time, prepared to tolerate an explosion of information exchange hitherto unimagined in China. This change had been forced on them by new social mobility within China and outside it; by a flourishing of print media and TV programming; and by the introduction into China of modern ICTs, especially mobile telephones (offering sms), computers, the internet (electronic file transfer, emails and bbs), and the world wide web (search engines). Yet several substantial exceptions to the more liberal environment for information exchange remained. The crackdown in 1999 on Falun Gong made it plain that the CCP would continue to intrude in matters of personal conscience of the most innocuous kind if they led to what looked remotely like organized activity on a mass scale that was not directly controlled by the CCP. Most importantly, there was no freedom of conscience when it came to political affairs that might even remotely impinge on the continued rule of the CCP. This even extended to scientific work that might run against the public lines of government policy. Thus, there was only freedom of information exchange within China in 1999 for personal affairs of no possible public consequence, and in pure science. There had been considerable liberalization in information exchange for economic planning, for applied sciences and for social sciences, with new levels of tolerance for open information. One positive example in this area was the blossoming of information about the degraded natural environment in China through industrial pollution. But for the most part, state secrecy and state ideology were the dominant values.

Protection of information exchange: The leaders' values on the circulation of information make it plain that in 1999 they did not place a high value on the principle of protecting the exchange of information. On the contrary, they showed a persistent commitment to punishing those who transgressed CCP guidelines. Since the legal system in China was weak at the time, there were few protections of any kind for citizens, activists or researchers in their confrontations with the CCP apparatus over access to information. Even if information that was circulated in no way impinged on political power, citizens had few protections. There were, however, signs of counter-currents, with the State Secrets Bureau in 1999 commissioning the country's first research on FOI regimes in other countries.

Trusted information: The leaders faced a dilemma on this front. On the one hand, the original attraction of the idea of an information economy for Deng Xiaoping was the need for China to have basic and accurate statistics and informed analysis about the entirety of life in China. This demanded accurate information that could be protected from ideological bias. By 1999, Chinese leaders were insisting on objective information in state planning. Yet, with the maintenance of heavy ideological control of content and tight control of mass media where possible, even on personal issues, there could be little confidence in much of the information in circulation in China. The state of play in the field by the end of the decade was captured in complaints by senior officials of falsification and exaggeration of economic data by their peers keen to preserve careers by being seen to meet economic targets.

Innovative information economy

Transformation intent: This was a supreme value for China's leaders. They wanted the country to become rich, strong, democratic and civilized – on a par with the developed countries. Yet, for political reasons, they were committed to a path that emphasized experimentation and gradual reform. This meant that bureaucratism and a slow pace of change were the norm. However, the leaders were capable of breakthrough decisions and there had been striking examples of these in the previous twenty years: the decision to set up special economic zones, the crafting of the political principle of 'one country, two systems', the decision to admit entrepreneurs to the Communist Party, the decision to allow public access to the internet, the initial listing of Chinese corporations on the New York Stock Exchange, and the agreement to United States terms for China to enter the World Trade Organization (WTO). Foreign corporations and governments also played a massively important role to enable such shifts in leadership values on the economic front, especially on the issue of closer integration of China into the global economy. By 1999, many indicators on the technological side in China's information economy were in take-off mode, with notable exceptions in industry being the software and semi-conductor sectors, which were verging on the negligible.

Innovation system: It was only towards the end of the 1990s that the leaders began to accept that a command economy, with strongly centralized ideological and social controls, was antithetical to innovation on the level needed to achieve an advanced information economy. The leaders had arrived at the turn of the century with a set of experiences in innovation policy that had given a central role to experiments or surge campaigns in dedicated (narrow) industrial or scientific sectors. There was no strong commitment to rapid reform of incentives or key institutions, though there was a deepening recognition of the need to engage market forces more directly. There was only reluctant acceptance of foreign expertise as the driver. Most leaders were clinging to the dream of self-reliance (a techno-nationalist vision). This was the belief, present at the start of the opening-up policy, that China only needed a little bit of stimulus from outside the country, and the superiority of its socialist system would kick in and carry China the rest of the way.

Innovator class: The brain drain from China was probably close to a forty-year peak around 1999. The phenomenon had been debated at the highest leadership levels for at least fifteen years. This reflected the lack of commitment by leaders to the value of developing an innovator class through deployment of competitive working conditions and an attractive social and intellectual environment. After 1949, China's entire economic history had been about a command economy, institutional targets and an education system that operated in an ideological straitjacket. There had been so little private sector development in the country that this was not a source of innovators. The leaders had placed considerable faith in a strategy that comprised sending scientists and scholars abroad to study, expectations for transfer of technology to China from foreign-invested firms in the country (including their R&D labs), and gradual improvements in tertiary and research institutes in the country. They had also relied on surge programmes for talent development in selected areas of technology, such as electronics and IT. The evolution of an innovator class was stunted by the leaders' unwavering commitment to CCP control of leadership posts in key research institutions and universities. Yet by 1999, entrepreneurship in information technology and services was alive and well in spite of leadership preferences. Completely new forms of internet-based business had emerged and the leaders did not discourage this.

Global information ecosystem

Strategic stability: From the earliest days of the reform period, China's foray into the knowledge economy was dependent on its diplomatic strategies and borrowing from foreign experts. By 1999, the leaders remained as firmly convinced as Deng Xiaoping had been in 1978 that advanced technology determines national power. Since China was badly lacking in it, then the only solution was to work cooperatively with foreign countries to get it. The leaders were highly committed to the idea that China should promote strategic stability, meaning peaceful and advantageous relations with the major economic powers and with foreign private investors, in order to underpin as rapid a modernization of the country as possible. They were, however, reluctant acceptors of the existing world order. As they modernized their armed forces and normalized their maritime boundaries, they were encountering strong suspicions from neighbouring countries about China's growing military and economic power. The leaders recognized a need to try to calm those anxieties. They saw themselves increasingly obliged to respond to the US drive for enduring pre-eminence over all other states in military technologies. While the leaders had committed fully to a high-tech vision of future warfare over the longer term, the extent of their potential commitment to military informatization was still being debated. The PLA by 1999 had started to develop only limited cyber war ideas and basic capabilities (beyond classic signals intelligence).

Bridging military divides: Part of China's peaceful development strategy was to oppose military alliances. But since the leaders placed a high premium on preventing the permanent separation of Taiwan from China, through use of military force if necessary, the strategic stand-off with Taiwan and its military ally, the United States, continued. China had from 1992 to 1995 promoted a series of peaceful gambits towards Taiwan, but this had flared into sustained military tensions between July 1995 and 1999. China's leaders were prepared to alienate Taiwanese investors and forego better access to advanced information technologies from Western countries through this occasional sabre-rattling, but in fact they found that foreign investment in China's ICT sector was continuing apace in spite of it.

Interdependent informatized security: China was committed in practice to cooperative norms in economic and technological aspects of the global information economy. It had shown an emerging rhetorical commitment to joint problem solving, but leadership values in this area in 1999 were limited almost totally to the idea that richer countries were obliged to help poorer countries (like China) acquire advanced information technologies. There was a very powerful 'China first' strategy. China was supplying low-interest development loans to some poor countries, but saw itself as so backward that it had to concentrate on its own national development.

CONCLUSION

Thus, across most domains of policy, the leaders of China in 1999 had highly conflicted values towards informatization of their economy and society. The main consequence of this was that the time-frame for coming closer to the goal became more protracted the more their values diverged from the ideal. The trajectory of China's informatization had been far from smooth. Another consequence was that each shortcoming in policy deepened the sense of frustration among the leaders because every time China slowed or stopped its course in key areas of policy, this allowed other countries to advance even farther ahead. Each political crackdown in China was a major setback to its efforts to enlist its intellectuals behind the information economy standard. As the turn of the century and the millennium approached, China's leaders had a choice: quicken the pace towards an information society and hold the line consistently – or fall farther behind.

3 | e-Democracy, i-Dictatorship

Around 2000, China experienced the biggest growth rate in internet-transmitted information over any twelve-month period before or since. This information explosion, like the opening of the Berlin Wall in 1989, has presented unprecedented 'life-changing' opportunities and threats to the Communist Party in respect of maintaining its hold on power. The pre-existing situation of information dictatorship (i-dictatorship) now had to co-exist with China's version of e-democracy. In a situation where the public display of a physical poster by a private citizen on a politically sensitive topic remained subject to severe recrimination, Chinese citizens by the year 2000 had, it seemed, been given the power to make electronic posters at will. This chapter addresses the evolution of leadership attitudes towards the emerging and quite unfamiliar information ecosystem in China. This is the first set of ideal values outlined in table 1.2: freedom of information exchange, the protection by law of information exchange, and the related value of information security and trust.

FREEDOM OF INFORMATION EXCHANGE IN THE SECRET STATE

In 2000, the Politburo determined that the information society would now become a primary goal of policy (Jiang 2010). The intent was to use information technology to achieve a 'leap forward' in social productivity. The Politburo started first to upgrade the economic information analysis assets that Deng Xiaoping had set his sights on back in 1984 when he linked the goal of informatization to the four modernizations. In January 2000, the MII officially approved a network called the China International Economy and Trade Net (CIETnet). In March, the Securities Regulatory Commission issued interim measures for online management of securities. In June, the China Electronic Commerce Association was created and in July the Enterprise Online project was set up (CNNIC 2013). The private sector was no longer a passive bystander. Sina.com, owned by a company registered in the United States, made an initial public offering through the New York Stock Exchange (followed by similar offerings by Sohu and Netease the same year). A private internet news consortium, *Qianlong*, was set up. The first Chinese search engine on the mainland, Baidu, was set up by private investors, led by two Chinese nationals returning from IT development work in the United States.

By 2000, the leaders of China were facing a progressive weakening of the monopoly over information dissemination they had worked so hard to nurture, and which they saw as central to their hold on power. As they took stock of this unfamiliar terrain, they could see that within ten years or so China would have more internet users than any other country and more internet users than the United States has people. The leaders also knew that quantitative measures of growth in hardware and platforms were in fact only a raw indicator of the trends in information exchange. The more staggering figures for a leadership intent on information control were those for the amount of new data created each day. For example, by 2000, the country's mobile phone users (about 100 million) were already sending around ten billion short messages in one year (Dai 2002).

One test of the leaders' commitment to exchange of information in 2000 was their approach at the time to FOI and open government. They were only prepared to take a baby step, with the decision to promote 'openness in government' at the township level. This came after a move in 1998 for the village level. (There are five levels of government in China below the national level, in descending hierarchy: province or municipality with provincial status, prefecture, county, township and village.) Both open government measures (village and township) were understood as promoting transparency in the interests of grassroots democracy. But the openness did not eventuate. The first township (in fact the first administrative unit in the entire country) to practise open government by releasing full budget details (Baimiao township in Sichuan province) did so only in 2010 (Xiao 2012). Few have followed. Another small step towards open government occurred in 2000 with provisions in a new law on legislation that set in place, in principle at least, a commitment to public consultation on draft laws. This has never been consistently consummated in practice either, but has become reasonably well established as a principle of legislative practice in China. The idea of an FOI system in China, where citizens could request government-held information, was beginning to take hold then as well. The first public research on FOI legislation for China had been done in 1999 at the behest of the Law Institute in the Chinese Academy of Social Sciences (CASS), in a project designed to help the State Secrets Bureau understand the limits of the evolving interest of high-level political leaders in more transparency (Xiao 2012).

Yet, in spite of these signs of new openness, the government still sought to retain a monopoly on the dominant news messages and leading information indicators about public life at the national level. In 2000, a number of dedicated, government-owned news websites appeared for the first time: people.com.cn, xinhuanet, china.com.cn, CCTV.com, CRI Online, China Daily and China Youth International (Wacker 2003). Presumably the ideological departments and public security agencies were also feeling less than satisfied with their ability to compete. The government-owned media were (and are still) ideological mouthpieces of the CCP.

The CCP upgraded the SILG in 2001 and put it under the premier, instead of a vice-premier. This body had from its founding in 1996 been a largely economic and technocratic organization, intended to oversee development of the information economy. Now that the goal had become one of an information society (as opposed to merely an information economy), there was a new need to politicize this high-level policy group. The SILG has been supported for routine matters by the State Council Informatization Office (SCITO). Though the SCITO had a powerful hand to play in areas like e-government or technical administration of the internet, it could not move on more sensitive issues without CCP and MPS control. SCITO policy analysis was supported by the Advisory Committee for State Informatization (ACSI), set up initially with three departments in its secretariat (policy, application and security). The ACSI provided the clearing house for all policy initiatives on their way into the SILG for approval and on their way out for implementation.

The following two years saw a further dramatic step-up in leadership policy settings to promote the information environment. Several individual agencies had begun issuing measures on making more administrative information public. At that time, similar national-level provisions had been drafted by the SILG, but not promulgated (Qu 2010).The leaders obviously could not agree that they wanted to go very far with more public access. At this very time, the ambition for transparency that underpinned an information society was held up to some ridicule among the Chinese public because of a government cover-up in 2002 and 2003 of the outbreak of the epidemic disease severe acute respiratory syndrome (SARS).

In one of the earliest moves by China towards open accountable government at the national level, the State Council in 2003 made its first release ever of a national audit report, unleashing an audit storm over the next year or two that evoked a massive amount of public interest. The audit report was held up by the government as an exercise in a new type of democratic supervision of government (Ling 2005). As a result of the findings, six officials of ministerial rank were charged with fraud-related offences and later convicted. Audits have continued to gain in stature and political significance in China as a form of government openness and as a vehicle for public scrutiny of official malfeasance and administrative effectiveness.

In 2004, the Politburo approved the first policy measures dedicated exclusively to the promotion of more rapid development of information resources that would inform policy decisions and help develop private sector economic interests (Qu 2010). Key elements of the policy included development of government information resources and mechanisms, developing public interest services, providing commercial information services for marketing, and improving the security environment. It emphasized three principles: transparency, sharing of information, and adding value in an economic sense (especially through private sector development).

Around this time, CCP leaders began to expound the concept of e-democracy with more frequency. This is the idea that public knowledge and public criticism of government policy through the internet are healthy and represent a new form of democracy. The idea was being held up by key leaders as the main plank of political reform being pursued by the CCP: that of consultative government and public supervision. They were presenting the new information freedom (opportunities for the public to react to government policies through the internet) as socialist democracy with Chinese characteristics. With the concept of e-democracy, the leaders of China were trying to represent the new voice possessed by the Chinese people through the internet as a continuation and deepening of the tradition of consultation embodied in the CPPCC, in place since 1949.

The government continued to monitor the flow of information very carefully while trying to promote its exploitation for economic advance. In 2005, some fourteen ministries and agencies, including Public

Security, Information Industry and Commerce, issued regulations on non-profit internet information services. Throughout 2005 and 2006, the government put in place the first measures for the entry of private capital into the 'cultural industry', laying out measures for digital radio, TV, films, publications, animation and network games (Qu 2010). The government made progress in setting up nationwide databases in many key areas of policy, including population, natural disasters, patents, environment and traditional Chinese medicine. Internet platforms were being used for distance education, especially at primary and secondary level, and for graduate employment (job seeking). The online gaming industry and digital film and TV production were in full swing.

By 2006, internet platforms to maximize information exchange and social networking on a par with those in the developed countries were all in place and, in most cases, had been for several years. Table 3.1 shows a list of start-up dates.

In a white paper on building political democracy in China, released in 2006, the government formally recognized for the first time at national level the role of open government in safeguarding democratic rights: the rights to know, to participate, to supervise and to express an

Table 3.1: Start-up dates for public Chinese internet platforms, 2000 onwards

BRAND NAME	PLATFORM TYPE	YEAR
Baidu	Search engine and MP3 site	2000
Taobao	Person-to-person sales	2003
Tianji	Professional social network	2005
Tudou	Video sharing	2005
Sina weibo	Microblog	2005
Xiaonei (RenRen)	Student social network	2005
Youku	Video sharing	2006

opinion (Xiao 2012). Yet by then, seven years after the launch of the national e-government project for all government agencies to set up websites, the agencies were on average receiving failing grades for website performance, with county-level agencies failing even more seriously (Qu 2010). That year, three Politburo members from the SILG, including the premier, Wen Jiabao, as chair of the SILG, told a work conference on national e-governance that the situation of information exchange in the country was still poor. The premier issued written instructions aiming 'to boost the reform of the administrative and management system, enhance government work efficiency and public service level, and create conditions for the public to participate in economic and social activities'. It was only in 2006 that a comprehensive national e-government strategy was devised and a centralized portal (www.gov.cn) was established. Its content was to be managed by Xinhuanet, the online arm of the official state news agency, and was to appear in traditional Chinese characters (for Taiwan and Hong Kong) alongside the simplified characters in use in the mainland, as well as in English.

In January 2007, building on earlier baby steps, China issued a regulation on the Open Government Initiative (OGI), which was an FOI measure for 'safeguarding the legal access to government information by citizens, legal persons and other organisations'. This set of regulations, as already mentioned, had been in draft since 2002 – the delay representing in itself the degree of opposition within parts of the leadership to open government of the most perfunctory kind. In addition to public access, the regulations had other declared purposes: improving the transparency of government work, promoting a law-based approach to public administration, and fostering the use of government information for analysis that would increase productivity, economic development and social welfare. Thus, what had been a tentative experimental step in 2000 with the township-level open government initiative was now, seven years later, being upgraded and extended nationwide (at least in principle). The measures entered into force in May the next year, presumably to allow departments and agencies to prepare for compliance. The regulations vest in government authorities the right of refusal but do provide for independent administrative review of refused requests through an administrative suit.

Even as the government issued new regulations on open government in 2008 and sent inspection teams around the country to review practices in place, eight ministries and administrative offices jointly released a set of 'opinions' intended to increase controls over internet maps and geographic information system (GIS) websites. As this example shows, an inevitable consequence of China's secrecy regime is that scholars and policy analysts are denied the basic building blocks of the scientific analysis that makes an information society.

For China's leaders from Deng Xiaoping onwards, the opening up of information about the country was supposed to be one of the essential aspects of the information reforms. Qu's (2010) assessment was that by 2008, in spite of considerable progress, there were 'still areas of concern' with e-governance: databases were very basic, integration of government information was not strong enough, and public interest information resources needed more attention. In a *Media Project* blog in Hong Kong around this time, one analyst aptly observed that while social media have very often filled a gap in reporting left by mainstream media, that had had the effect of depriving Chinese of 'substantive information and cool-headed analysis' (Qin 2007).

One of the few motors for continuing reform in government openness, the Centre for Public Participation Studies and Supports (CPPSS) at Beijing University, began in 2009 to publish what was intended to be an annual assessment of the openness of Chinese government agencies. (The centre had been set up three years earlier.) With central government support, the CPPSS created an OGI Index Assessment Center to develop an appropriate review system, to prepare a watch report, to prepare a citizens' guide on OGI, and to edit a monthly magazine called *Transparency*. According to CNNIC, 2009 was a good year for promoting public supervision through the internet, with a number of high-profile cases of exposure of official malfeasance (CNNIC 1986–2013). Citizens or journalists were increasingly using the internet, often anonymously, to expose the behaviour of corrupt officials or other miscreants, with such exposure leading to their arrest.

Also in 2009, the premier Wen Jiabao became the second Chinese leader to directly interact with netizens of China when he participated in a two-hour question-and-answer session jointly hosted by Xinhuanet and gov.cn, the government's official portal (*China Daily* 28/02/2008). (CCP general secretary Hu had undertaken a brief Q&A with netizens through the *People's Daily* website the previous year.) Wen staked a lot in his remarks on open government and public consultation, including his assertion that officials should declare their assets. He said the government was making active preparations for such declarations as a way of preventing corruption.

China published a white paper on the internet in 2010, an event that came a full fifteen years after the technology began to be introduced publicly. One of the primary motivations for publishing the white paper was to set out the public values around use of the internet. The white paper affirms freedom of speech, democratic supervision of government policies and the citizens' constitutional right to know: 'Vigorous online ideas exchange is a major characteristic of China's Internet development.' The paper reported that 'The leaders of China frequently log onto the Internet to get to know the public's wishes, and sometimes have direct online communication with netizens to discuss state affairs and answer their questions.'

The National Audit Office was becoming a major player in openness by scandal. In 2012, its just-released performance report for the previous year identified 38 cases of corruption uncovered in the previous three years and reported that, in 2011 alone, some 1,577 cases were handed over by the Audit Office to the judicial and disciplinary inspection and supervision organs, involving 2,395 people (www.cnao. gov). The total value of public funds used illegally in 2011 was just under RMB500 billion, a staggering figure.

The debate on open government had become public, wide-ranging and intense. In 2012, it came to involve CCP leaders directly, after publication of the stories by United States news outlets (*New York Times* and Bloomberg) on the personal wealth of the immediate family members of Wen Jiabao and Xi Jinping. After Wen said in reaction that he was prepared to disclose his personal assets, there were public calls for other Chinese leaders to do the same. While CCP provincial authorities in Guangdong indicated that they would lead, and some new measures were introduced in Hong Kong, China's central leadership did not embrace this proposal.

The current limits of leadership attitudes to transparency can be seen clearly in the sixty-point reform agenda released after the Third Plenum of the 18th Congress of the CCP in November 2013. One sub-point reads: 'Explore moving forward with openness of State-owned enterprise finance and budgeting, and other such important information.' The invocation is to explore the possibility, not actually to do it yet.

The limits of open government in China have been revealed in several high-profile cases that illustrate the way in which the OGI regulation is limited by other laws, including the law on state secrets, and by other regulations. One of the most notable is the decision communicated on 1 February 2013 from China's Ministry of Environmental Protection that the data from a national survey on soil pollution conducted in 2010 could not be made public because of state secrecy laws (Dong 2013). But state secrecy has also been imposed in other less formalized processes, with few recent cases being more prominent than the efforts by Chinese authorities to prevent the public from learning the death toll from the earthquake in Sichuan province in May 2008. In this disaster, more than 5,000 school students were killed, in part as the result of the shoddy construction of the buildings, an outcome that is likely to have resulted from corruption by local officials accepting bribes to overlook substandard completion. The people who tried to establish the death toll in the first year after the earthquake, including famous artist and designer Ai Weiwei, have been subjected to physical harassment, beatings, illegal detention, internet censorship and surveillance. These two cases indicate very clearly that for the Chinese bureaucratic apparatus, information can on occasions be treated as the enemy.

By 2013, the sheer volume and speed of information exchange in China, including information on state persecution of political activists or other hapless victims of administrative abuse, had defied totalitarian control of the traditional kind. China, with a population of 1.3 billion, had more telephone subscriptions than people and more registered internet users (people and organizations) than any other country in the world. The state monopoly on publishing that existed in the 1980s has been blown apart, though all private publishers still have to be licensed in some way. As the following section of the chapter recounts, all are subject to political censorship and review, even if that happens after the fact rather than before.

The leaders have not succumbed to this pressure for relaxation of control. They could not by 2013 commit to open government on any substantial level. The CCP budget was 100 per cent unrevealed. The annual budgets for defence and internal security were still reported with only a very broad breakdown of main categories, to the extent that both are repeatedly the subject of wild misinterpretation by scholars inside and outside China. It was only in January 2013 that the PLA revealed that the unit designation for the group armies in China would no longer be a state secret (*People's Daily Online* 16/01/2013). (The irony of this is that for at least two decades the group army designations, their locations and their commanders had been public knowledge outside China.)

The stop–start, restrictive, reactive or baby-step profile of CCP policies on certain types of information exchange after 2000 has to be understood against the background of the ideological opening up of information flow among the intelligentsia and creative classes. Apart from information questioning the continued rule of the CCP, revealing sensitive actions by its leaders or officials or running contrary to key ideological campaigns (against Falun Gong or the Roman Catholic Church), most of the ideological constraints of former decades have gradually evaporated. More courageous people in the two main Chinese academies (CASS and CAS) led their own information revolution, in part because the CCP officials in key watchdog posts within the academies had adopted an increasingly hands-off approach to information flow and content. This transition was initially more evident behind closed doors than in public, but even this distinction evaporated too. In advanced research institutes and their publications, almost all opinions are tolerated – except those that advocate concrete action to change China's political system. That said, researchers who express more radical opinions (by Chinese standards) or who conduct challenging research can be effectively marginalized through administrative measures, such as dismissal from the university. Loyalty to a broadly defined, non-specific set of CCP values is essential for promotion in most institutions, the majority of which are led by CCP members.

One notable exception to the CCP's tolerance of the open exchange of ideas in research or academic settings is the student body in universities. They remain a focus of leadership attention because of past student opposition movements and rising cynicism inside universities about the CCP. University curricula and teaching methods are for the most part ideologically constrained by the CPP anyway. Yet, even in this environment, the CCP regularly issues instructions to limit discussion of sensitive ideas. This is precisely what happened sometime in early 2013 when news broke of a directive to lecturers not to discuss 'universal values, freedom of the press, a civil society, civic rights, historical mistakes committed by the Communist Party, elite cronyism, and an independent judiciary' (*China Digital Times* 10/05/2013 reporting the *South China Morning Post*). The report was originally leaked by a Weibo account. On a more serious level, in December 2012, a university professor associated with a new activist group called the China Democracy Party was forcibly incarcerated in a mental hospital, reportedly to prevent his further activism (RFA 2012).

The instruction mentioned in the previous paragraph may be linked to a 'Circular Concerning the Present Situation in the Ideological Area' issued by the CCP for study and action by its ideological workers. The document is tightly held, and paper copies may not be removed from offices where it has been distributed. As a media monitor project reports, 'many blog posts or forum discussions referring to this document have been taken down' (CC&M 2013). The mood of the leaders was revealed in April 2013, when one day after the *New York Times* received a media prize for its reporting on the wealth of the extended family of Wen Jiabao, Xinhua issued a strong and regressive measure: 'All news outlets are not allowed to use news information from foreign media or foreign websites without permission.' The instruction required news organizations with a Weibo account to report to the authorities for the record and to appoint a staff person to be responsible for 'posting authoritative information and deleting harmful information in time' (Reporters without Borders 17/04/2013). According to the Reporters without Borders press freedom index of 2013, China sits among the ten worst performers: 173rd out of 179 countries. (The United States is ranked 32nd.)

The CCP measures could not prevent the emergence, recurrence and escalation of information campaigns by civil society organizations or news outlets against government policies. One example is the campaign in 2010 led by a number of independent-leaning state media outlets through their editorials calling for significant reform of the household registration system. (Household registration is a process that determines a person's access to social services and social support for dependent family members, especially education for children. It discriminates between rural and urban workers, especially against the rural migrant workers in the major cities.) A leading figure in the activist group was dismissed as a result and the editorial was taken down from websites (Minzer 2010). Yet by November 2013, further though limited reforms to the system had been announced for second-level cities in China. This is a good example of the consistent tension between critique, repression and policy change. In some cases, it can be assumed that journalists, academics or others often venture a criticism on behalf of a CCP leader who is trying to advance (or oppose) reform in a particular area or policy.

PROTECTING INFORMATION EXCHANGE, OR THE i-DICTATORSHIP

China's leaders had prepared their defences for this information explosion long ago. The agency in China with the highest responsibility for security since 1980 has been the Central Political and Legal Commission (CPLC) of the CCP. It had been replaced briefly in 1988, at the height of the liberalization, by a Leading Small Group. In May 1990, after the Tiananmen crackdown, the CPLC was re-established. It is responsible for supervising policy and delivery of results in all aspects of internal security across the executive, the judiciary and legislature in one unified system subject to full political control from the CCP. The CPLC supervises the MPS, the MSS, the Ministry of Justice, the courts, the police and the preparation of all legislation. In concert with the CMC of the Party, the CPLC commands and supervises the operations and planning for the People's Armed Police (PAP), based on units decommissioned from the PLA in the 1980s and having responsibility as a paramilitary force for internal security and border security. The PAP's internal security forces comprise fourteen mobile divisions

(140,000 troops) and guards troops (400,000 personnel whose responsibilities include leadership security).

The scale of CPLC power can be illustrated in many ways. In simple bureaucratic terms, its head had from 1980 to 2012 been a senior member of the Politburo, often holding several posts simultaneously that reached across different organizational realms, thereby making him exceptionally powerful. Cheng Li (2012) describes how, at a lecture in Beijing, two of China's most active proponents of legal reform, He Weifang and Xu Xin, had characterized the power of the CPLC as near infinite, with He alluding to the 'invisible hand' of the CPLC in 'recent well known cases of injustice'.

Under the CPLC, the most powerful organization with an influence on information society policy has been the MPS. Its most powerful arm in information society policy appears to be the 11th Bureau, which has responsibility for supervision of the security of all public information networks. The bureau is the lead organization in electronic monitoring of information exchange in China. According to a Falun Gong organization operating outside China, it was in the year 2000 that a Chinese software company, Haitian, on behalf of the MPS (presumably the 11th Bureau), entered into a joint venture with Microsoft China to develop technology for monitoring dissident or unacceptable traffic inside China and from abroad, including Voice of America radio (WOIPFG 2005).

Internet censorship and monitoring, discussed later in this section, have become one the CPLC's main functions, but that is only one of many ways in which the CPLC and MPS influence is brought to bear on the information society. Through its seat as a vice-chair of the SILG and through its main administrative arm, the MPS, the CPLC has been able to veto or retard progress in all other aspects of policy that might materially affect China's information society ambition. These include education policy, technology choices, encryption standards, foreign trade, and legal regimes for foreign investment decisions (and their enforcement or non-enforcement). All the MPS has to do is claim a domestic security interest.

By February 2014, the SILG had been transformed in two ways. Xi Jinping became the first general secretary of the CCP to sit as its chair, while simultaneously announcing that a much higher priority would be attached to informatization policy. At the same time, the name and priorities of the group seemed to change, giving an even higher security and political complexion to policy in this area than had existed previously. Its new name was reported as the Central Leading Group for Cybersecurity and Informatization (Xinhua 27/02/2014).

So how did leadership views of protection of the information dictatorship, working through this omnipresent set of watchdog organizations, develop after the turn of the century?

In 2000, the general secretary of the CCP, Jiang Zemin, made a speech to the CMC on the need for more attention to be paid to informatization because 'sovereignty of information' had now become an issue and the internet had become a new ideological and political battleground. It was in 2000 that the leaders took an important step to deepen the politicization and securitization of the SILG by making it a Party leading group (while keeping the nomenclature of a state leading group). The work of its local equivalents across the country also changed after that time (Yang Fengchun 2009).

China set up its first National Computer Network Emergency Response Technical Team Coordination Center (CNCERT) in 2000, and this was to become the focal point of national security management as well as international interaction on internet administration. While such a body might in other countries serve largely technical purposes, CNCERT would also serve as the hub for political control of the internet by the CPLC. A number of security-related laws and regulations were issued in 2000: the NPC Standing Committee Decision on Safeguarding Internet Security, bringing the internet explicitly under the preserve of the Administrative Penalties for Public

Security; measures for the Administration of Internet Information Services; and the entry into force of Administrative Provisions on the Maintenance of Secrets in the International Networking of Computer Information Systems, a decree issued by the State Secrets Bureau. It was also in 2000 that Chinese provinces, beginning with Anhui, started to set up a specialized Internet Police Force. In 2000, the CCP issued detailed instructions for banned content on the internet, which were identical to instructions for banned content for print media issued in 1997 (Wacker 2003).

The political system in which the dialogue about the future of China's information society was conducted from 2000 onwards had to be optimized for control while still allowing for innovation. At around this time, the PSC made a decision that the CCP could only contain the effects of the internet through tight social control rather than through heavy state censorship of the sort foreshadowed in George Orwell's novel *Nineteen Eighty-Four*. The CCP now had to rely on a larger network of co-opted monitors inside a range of business entities and other administrative authorities who would be charged with censorship and other technical controls of the internet on behalf of the state. The decision was implemented through the newly established Internet Society of China, which immediately began asking internet service providers (ISPs) and other organizations to sign a voluntary commitment to censor what the government regarded as inappropriate, whether for political, anti-crime or social morality reasons.

In 2001, when the upgraded SILG met under the premier (then Zhu Rongji), other Politburo members joined the group for the first time, for the purpose of providing 'stronger leadership to the promotion of informatization and to the safeguarding of state information security' (www.asci.gov.cn/en). At this time, the new vice-chairs had backgrounds that were more political and propaganda-related than security-related. This turn in policy towards greater securitization of the internet was manifested in part by the establishment in 2002 of a new committee to coordinate the security of state information and networks (Qu 2010). At this time, the MPS was reported to have 18,000 dedicated information and communications police, with basic data on 1.1 billion citizens in its computer systems, and more detailed information available on around 600 million of them (Cisco 2002).

The leaders were quite content to buy the security services they needed from foreign corporations, and in 2002 Cisco seemed to be closely involved in negotiations with the MPS, as had Microsoft before it. This sort of relationship (which could provide the best available technologies, subject in some cases to export controls) gave the leaders strong confidence that they could shore up their policy of social control with the best IT hardware and software for internal security. The confidence was underpinned by rapid growth rates in the number of students admitted each year for university-level study of 'public security technology' between 1999 and 2002.

The following year, 2003, saw the further securitization of the SILG when Zhou Yongkang (later to become head of the CPLC) became minister of public security and a vice-chair in the SILG. It was at this point that the security aspects of China's information policy took an even sharper turn. That year, the SILG approved the Recommendation on the Strengthening of Information Security Protection. One insight into the mood at the time can be seen in a 2003 document from Shaanxi province cited by a Falun Gong organization (WOIPFG 2005). Referring to the '610 Offices', a unit of the government set up exclusively to suppress Falun Gong, the document reads: 'The Party committees of schools must solidly intensify the leadership over the Internet struggle . . . 610 Offices of the schools should fully cooperate with the school Internet control units . . . strictly forbid people in the schools and especially "Falun Gong" members to visit "Falun Gong" websites.'

The intention of the MPS to exploit advanced information technology to the full was demonstrated in 2004 when it decided to set up a grid-based surveillance system in sensitive parts of Beijing, such as areas around Tiananmen Square. The system combined visual and internet-based surveillance, and relied on a team of six or seven people per grid to monitor groups of around 1,500 people. Reports are sent in by mobile phone and monitored in a sub-district office (*Economist* 2013). Also in 2004, the government set up the China Internet Illegal Information Reporting Centre (CIIRC), supported by the MPS and other agencies. This was part of the Communist Party's reliance on social controls. It uses the CIIRC to enable public supervision of all internet activity. That year China almost doubled its intake of students in bachelor's courses for public security technology compared with the previous year, and the 2004 intake was 550 per cent higher than that for 1999.

The CCP had made control of the internet a very high political priority. In 2007, the general secretary, Hu Jintao, told a meeting of the Politburo that 'Whether we can cope with the Internet is a matter that affects the development of socialist culture, the security of information, and the stability of the state' (*China Daily* 25/01/2007). This sentiment has never been far from the minds of China's leaders since the internet was introduced into China. But they have exhibited a consistent determination to control the new medium to prevent the overthrow of the one-party state, and they have shown a high degree of confidence that they could control it. Leading American corporations, such as Google, Microsoft and Yahoo!, had been accused the year before by Amnesty International of being complicit in Chinese government censorship (AI 2006).

When the new Central Committee was appointed according to the five-yearly timetable in 2007, the SILG had a large leadership core of five Politburo members, representing a far more powerful constellation of political power in the SILG than in 2000. No other country in the world had probably concentrated so many of its highest political leaders in a committee for informatization. The SILG contained other members below Politburo rank from different organizations and ministries. What is also remarkable about this structure by 2007 was the heavy representation of security, military and propaganda institutional interests relative to that for technology, education or scientific interests. Beyond the premier, there were no scientific, technological or education interests represented at leadership level in the peak body even though some twenty-five ministries participated in its work at lower levels. There also appears to have been little sign of private sector or civil society representation, in contrast to their highly visible presence in corresponding high-level bodies in many other countries.

Each innovation in information exchange, such as the introduction by Sina in 2009 of a Twitter-like service, Weibo, created new peaks in usage to which the information dictatorship had to adapt. But such daunting changes only strengthened the determination of leaders to stick with entrenched principles. In 2009 and 2010, a number of official statements revealed an intensifying focus on control of the internet and online communities, with the operational goal of striking early and preventing the snowballing of any unrest (CECC 2010). The leaders called on MPS personnel to 'place greater priority on correctly guiding online public sentiment'. The Party started a second phase of the Golden Shield project, the IT-based public security project for automated monitoring of all public security affairs (political dissent and crime) and automated record-keeping about citizens (dissenters and criminals alike). The new phase would emphasize command and control enhancements to increase coordination between local, provincial and national authorities for crisis or sensitive events, such as protest demonstrations.

The white paper on the internet in China, issued in 2010, reported that the CCP had set up 'informant websites', thereby reminding the public that someone would always be watching – as most Chinese already knew. As liberating as the internet might be, the CCP was in this way in 2010 simply reaffirming that the Party was going to use the internet as an instrument of control.

In 2011, the Chinese government issued a white paper on China's legal system, reaffirming that China is a 'people's democratic dictatorship'. Over more than a decade of struggle in the new information world, the preferences and values of the leaders as a collectivity had not changed and had not even wavered. They found that their ambition for political dictatorship could tolerate and survive a massive liberalization of media activity and information exchange (Esarey and Xiao 2011). By 2012, the number of dedicated internet police had reached 30,000, according to an informed source from a Western intelligence agency. But the bulk of the censorship effort did not lie with them. Rather, it lay with a larger number of censors or internet monitors operating within ISPs and within all institutions reliant on state support or subject to CCP direction.

Censorship was moving with the times. Even though the leaders had opted for a policy of social control over the internet after 2001, they had obviously pursued technical means as well. The process has been unrelenting, with budgets for the MPS rising steadily ever since. A project at Hong Kong University, called Weiboscope, identified 200 million posts deleted by the authorities or their proxies between 2011 and May 2013 (Chiu 2013). A study of the speed of take-downs of sensitive material by internet censors targeting Sina Weibo found that almost 30 per cent of the total deletion events occurred within 5–30 minutes, and almost 90 per cent of the deletions were happening within the first 24 hours (Zhu et al. 2013). The study showed that discussion of sensitive topics is short-lived, indicating that the CCP has established a capability to stop the 'viral' spread of hot issues. As reported by *Time Magazine* in 2009, after Uighur protesters rioted in Wulumuqi (Urumqi), leaving 200 people dead, the government restricted internet access in Xinjiang, blocked Twitter and Facebook, and closed down a microblog service called Fanfou (Ramzy 2011).

The CCP had decided on a more tightly focused criterion for its censorship: the potential for an internet activity to stimulate or promote undesirable collective action (King et al. 2013). This meant that the subject of an internet discussion was itself not seen as being as important as whether the discussion indicated plans for group organization of public action, protests or meetings.

A necessary corollary of the dominating status of the CPLC over the information society throughout this period was the weak rule of law. The overall policy setting on information policy from the top down was not FOI but control of it in order to contain political reform. This set of values was summarized by a member of the PSC, Wu Bangguo, who in 2011 as chairman of the country's NPC (the legislature) famously declared the Party's continuing commitment to its dictatorship. This has come to be known as the "Five No's" policy: 'we have made a solemn declaration that we will *not*: employ a system of multiple parties holding office in rotation; diversify our guiding thought; separate executive, legislative and judicial powers; use a bicameral or federal system; carry out privatisation' (Wu 2011).

Yet by mid-2012, the future of the CPLC was under a cloud because of the emergence of a phenomenon referred to in the press as 'internet terror'. The CPLC chief Zhou Yongkang had been identified as a political ally of the ousted Politburo member Bo Xilai, who had been implicated in serious violations of Party discipline, large-scale corruption and a brutal crackdown on criminality in Chongqing that caused widespread resentment. Of special note is that Bo had been accused in some reports of using advanced technologies to monitor the conversations of other Party leaders. Their suspicion would be that he had too much help in that from people under Zhou's control. One of these was the head of the Public Security Bureau in Chongqing, who was subsequently jailed for fifteen years for abuse of power, defection to the US consulate in Chengdu and taking bribes. The unfolding of this case coincided with the publication in two US news outlets of separate stories of the wealth of the immediate families of senior leaders, Wen Jiabao and Xi Jinping. The detailed listing of the assets of the two families was only made possible by internet search of records in China (including Hong Kong) and elsewhere. And the censors in China could not completely block dissemination of the story there. Thus in two separate ways (new technical surveillance of private conversations and the blasting out in public of private information) the leaders came to feel directly the same internet terror that ordinary Chinese had been feeling about their exposure to similar threats. In late 2012, responding perhaps to a speech by Xi Jinping on the need for firmer measures against corruption, public use of internet exposure implicated three senior leaders (two ministers and one Politburo member) in separate cases of nepotism, false representation and corruption (Cheng Li 2013). It may have been no coincidence that by December that year, one month after the new CCP leadership was appointed, the Standing Committee of the NPC approved regulations on internet privacy (protection of electronic data) that had been stalled for more than a decade after they were first issued in draft.

The new CPLC appointed after the 18th CCP Congress in 2012 was led by a new secretary, Meng Jianzhu, who had been public security minister and who remained as a Politburo member. His replacement as minister, Guo Shengkun, was named as deputy secretary of the CPLC. In its first meeting in December 2012 after the Congress, Meng called on his subordinates to boost their capabilities in social communications in the new media era (Xinhua 18/12/2012). In April 2013, Meng returned to the theme of how the security agencies could use the internet to promote their interests, especially through good public relations programmes (Xinhua 26/04/2013). The news report mentioned that the Sina Weibo site of the Beijing Police already had 4.87 million followers, a rather staggering number. Whether this high figure illustrates community trust or suspicion, or more pragmatic considerations like traffic updates, is unclear. But it does reveal the potential reach of the CCP in social co-option of Chinese netizens.

In the sixty-point policy reform agenda released after the Third Plenum of the CCP in November 2013, the leaders committed yet again to 'expand forces to manage the network according to the law, accelerate the perfection of leading structures for Internet management, guarantee the security of the national network and of information'. In this section on social governance, they also endorsed the establishment of a National Security Committee, with a mission to 'perfect national security structures and national security strategies, and guarantee national security'. The establishment within the framework of public security of yet another high-level committee is a reliable indicator of deepening leadership concern about their ability to control the internet. Every few years, beginning in 1993/1994, they have created some new mechanism like this as an add-on to pre-existing committees or leading groups on internal security. On this occasion, however, the leaders will have been motivated by several factors. The most important may have been concern over the extreme power of the CPLC under Zhou Yongkang. Another consideration would have been the sense of vulnerability to foreign electronic espionage as a result of revelations by Edward Snowden, the former US National Security Agency employee who, beginning in June 2013, leaked hundreds of thousands of classified documents on US and allied cyber espionage. A third factor would have been the rapidly accelerating social unrest, facilitated in part by access to the internet and by internet-associated exposes of official misdeeds. The leaders' sense of insecurity is also evident in new measures announced around the same time to require every one of China's 200,000 journalists to pass a written test on Party ideology if they wanted to retain their press accreditation.

By 2013, the leaders' view of social control of the internet had become more nuanced. But its intent was perfectly clear. Some of the nuances that were emerging were summarized well in an interview with Fu Siming, a scholar in the Politics and Law Department at the Central Party School, published in *Study Times*, one of the school's journals (Bandurski 2013). In a five-point formula, Fu called for building a sound legal system (including industry self-regulation); using the internet to improve relations between the government and the public; ensuring public access to authoritative information and observance of the principle of OGI; making the ability to conduct network politics a necessary qualification for political leaders; and the effective channelling of public opinion, especially in connection with fast-breaking events.

As of 2013, according to a senior official, successful outcomes in criminal investigations were made possible in more than half of all crimes solved because of the use of technical surveillance data in MPS operations (Mattis 2013). While not without challenges, like inadequate training and bureaucratic turf wars, the enhanced effectiveness of the MPS surveillance through informatization is illustrated by a report of the large number of informants who feed information into the automated systems. Mattis (2011) cites several reports: one county-level MPS with a 12,000-person informant network out of a total local population of 400,000, pensioners assigned to watch for 'unstable elements', and intelligence units operating within universities.

Political dissidents, such as the Nobel Peace Prize winner Liu Xiaobo, or public interest activists like the artist Ai Weiwei, have not been able to garner significant public support against the implacable resistance of the CCP. It now has the biggest political and social apparatus in history for monitoring and controlling the social organization and distribution of information activities and the technologies that support them. As reported in July 2013, Xinhua carried the following exhortation: 'China's historical experience has shown over and over again that the nation's long-term stability can only be secured by protecting the authority of the central leadership' (SCMP 26/07/2013). This is still the leaders' highest value in terms of information exchange, and it trumps any consideration of protecting such exchange (FOI) for its own sake.

TRUSTED INFORMATION

In the environment sketched so far, with political control such a dominating force, and exchange of essential information on public policy quite restricted, it may be difficult to imagine a commitment by the leaders to building an ecosystem of trust in cyberspace. In fact their version of trust in cyberspace has focused very heavily on combating cyber crime, ensuring national security, and setting national standards for security of information systems. When they have addressed broader issues of social trust, they have focused most heavily on the need to prevent false information and rumours, especially about the CCP, from being spread via new media.

The leaders have had to deal with the same set of cyber crime problems faced by other countries. Chinese leaders see several factors making the environment in China even more challenging than that in the United States, Japan or the European Union, which are themselves struggling to cope with rampant cyber crime. First, the legal system in China is weakly developed, having been fully subordinated to political considerations at the whim of the leadership at all levels until quite recently. Second, the enforcement of existing law is subject to widespread corruption. Third, the education base for a workforce skilled in information technology skills appropriate to fighting cyber crime, or even to basic IT levels, has only reached a mass scale in the last five to ten years.

In 2000, in his speech at the World Computer Congress, Jiang Zemin advocated an international convention to promote internet security against cyber crime. Otherwise, the leaders were not saying anything too specific about this topic at the time. That year, a government-led National Information Security Report graded China at 5.5 on a scale of 9 (the highest level of security) – between relatively secure and slightly insecure (Qu 2010). The grading may have been a little optimistic. The report indicated that only 180 financial crimes in China had been perpetrated via the internet by 2000, while in 1999 alone there had been more than 900 attacks on financial networks. In the same year, the Standing Committee of the NPC approved a set of measures on internet security, and the MPS issued a set of measures for the prevention and control of computer viruses. Overall, the country was poorly placed to address the challenges of cyber crime even though the MPS had been active over the previous decade in laying the legislative groundwork.

A year later, in connection with a crackdown on unregistered internet cafés, the MPS (joined by the MII, the Ministry of Culture, and the State Administration for Industry & Commerce) released regulations on ISPs. The Measures on the Administration of Business Sites of Internet Access Services were regarded as so important and urgent that they came into force immediately. They provided the legal foundation for an immediate campaign of 'rectifications' against internet cafés. The China Information Technology Security Evaluation Center was formally approved by the government, two years after it had started operation. The central government joined with the Shanghai municipality to launch an S&T park devoted exclusively to developing a stronger domestic information security industry.

In part to counter cyber crime (though for political control as well), China in 2002 made the first moves to introduce a real-name registration system for internet users. Despite occasional claims that it has been successful, and completed, it clearly has not been, even more than a decade later. One of the main obstacles has been the sheer size of the population of internet users and the lack of effective control over the large number of ISPs, which are reluctant to commit the funds to undertake the registration consistently. Another constraint on implementation of the real-name system has been widespread public opposition, revealed in public opinion polls (Farrall 2008).

In 2003, the SILG made a significant fresh move when it released 'Opinions on Strengthening Information Security' (Qu 2010). These opinions, issued in the joint name of the Communist Party Central Committee and the State Council, were as political and social as they were technical or counter-crime in asserting several principles: protecting opening up and reform, balancing development and security, seeing management and technology as equally important avenues of security policy, boosting informatization and protecting the interests of the general public. With MPS involvement, work proceeded on setting up a risk assessment process and a graduated protection system.

It was not until 2005 that the Chinese government announced that all ministries and agencies should have a Chief Information Officer (CIO), a role that had emerged in the United States in most large organizations by the late 1980s, and which by the early 1990s was becoming an executive role (usually with a mix of responsibilities, ranging from strategic management of IT assets to maximizing exploitation of information resources and ensuring the security of IT systems and services.) That year, China's law on electronic signatures entered into force. For information professionals like Qu Weizhi, this was the country's first informatization law (Qu 2010). It controlled the use of and authentication processes for e-signatures, and associated measures for information security. The government also set up in 2005 a National Administrative Committee for Certification of Information Security Products (from the private sector).

Through 2005 and 2006, the government launched information security risk assessments in two cities (Beijing and Shanghai), two provinces (Heilongjiang and Yunnan) and more than twenty agencies, including the People's Bank of China (PBoC) and the State Grid (Qu 2010). Agencies involved in this process included the National Administration for the Protection of State Secrets, the State Cypher

Code Administration and SCITO. In 2006, the State Council promulgated Opinions on the Development of the Internet Credibility System, which set 2011 as the target date for achieving an effective information security national system (Qu 2010). By the close of the year, the government had completed work on a national network credit system with appropriate standards for authentication.

New security measures followed almost every year. In 2009, seven key ministries or commissions, led by the MPS, the State Council Information Office, the Ministry of Industry and Information Technology (MIIT) and the MoC, turned the spotlight on governance of vulgarity on the internet. The Office of the National Campaign on Anti-Prostitution and Anti-Delinquency issued an emergency notice to take down mobile website production and the spreading of obscene and pornographic information. As a result, the government carried out 'special actions' to reduce obscene, pornographic and vulgar information on the internet and mobile media.

Cyber crime was slowly coming more sharply into focus. In 2011, in China's biggest ever public breach of data, the stored information (username, password and email address) of 6 million users in the Computer Software Development Network in China were leaked and posted to the internet. The perpetrator was caught six months later.

In May 2012, an executive meeting of the State Council chaired by the premier, Wen Jiabao, approved a series of Proposals on Boosting Informatization and Safeguarding Information Security. On security, the State Council laid an emphasis on combining designs, construction and operation of important systems and networks with those of security protection facilities, improving infrastructure for network and information security, strengthening monitoring and early warning, and increasing reliance on research and development (Xinhua 10/05/2012). Two months later, police in China arrested a gang of fourteen cyber criminals involved in hacking government websites to allow them to make false certificates using stolen government seals. An official at the time said the crimes might have been avoided if the government policy of real-name registration for IP addresses had been fully implemented (*China Daily* 26/07/2012).

Yet for all the measures, the practice of information security (outside of the security services) in China remains weak. The size of the country, its overall developmental level in education and information technology, and the mass numbers of machines, networks, websites and users have presented daunting challenges. The effect of these underlying structural factors has been complicated by several other problems. For example, a large percentage of users in the country were using pirated Microsoft software that would not receive security patches (updates). Furthermore, many users were still using Internet Explorer 6.0, which had an unusually high number of known vulnerabilities. A snapshot of the situation at the end of 2012 could be seen in the Annual Report of CNCERT:

- 14 million IP addresses infected by Trojans or Botnets (an increase of 64.7 per cent over 2011)
- China's share of new infections by the Conficker virus per month the highest of any country in the world
- an increase of website defacements by 6.1 per cent compared with 2011
- 52,000 websites attacked by malware, with backdoors allowing remote control
- 22,000 thousand phishing sites targeting banks, with 96.2 per cent of the IPs used being outside China (80 per cent of them hosted in the United States)
- 58,000 backdoor control IP addresses
- 163,000 mobile computing and telephone malware samples collected. (CNCERT 2013)

Thus by 2014, almost twenty years after the internet first came to the public in China, there was something of a contradiction in play on the issue of security and trust. The world's biggest community of netizens was prepared to use the networks and machines, and consume the data, on a mass scale in spite of overall weak technical standards in the security environment, weak law enforcement against cyber criminals, and the certain knowledge that the government and its proxies were able read their email, SMS and tweets. So how can we understand the contours of trust inside China's information ecosystem and how can we understand the leaders' commitment to it?

There have been many surveys trying to understand the nuances of this situation. Trust in the ICT sector in China was not high at the outset. Snell and Tseng (2002) documented low levels of trust in 'network capitalism' through surveys in industrial enterprises. They attributed their results to a weak legal system, weak civic accountability, crony capitalism, public cynicism and a disempowered workforce. A longitudinal survey from 2000 to 2005 by the World Internet Project in partnership with the CASS showed that 'trust among Internet users in the reliability of online content has decreased significantly over the five years' (CASS 2007). The same survey found that users in China trusted non-internet foreign media news more than online news (regardless of the origin of the online news). Less than 50 per cent of the respondents believed content on the internet was reliable, and they saw it more as an entertainment (or infotainment) location than an information location. In a 2009 survey, China recorded a more trusting response: it had the highest level of confidence (54 per cent of respondents) among the participating countries that about half of the information available on the net was reliable, while another 32 per cent thought most of it was reliable (WIP 2009). In 2011, the *People's Daily Online* reported results of survey-based research suggesting that local government and central government websites (the latter including *People's Daily Online* and Xinhuanet) both fell into the low-trust category. Commercial websites, such as Sina.com and Sohu.com, received the lowest rank, 'indicating that the respondents have little trust in them'

(*People's Daily Online* 05/05/2011). In early 2013, the CASS released its annual 'blue book' (academic research compendium) on social mentality, which included survey results indicating that trust levels in China had dropped to a record low and that, while having low levels of trust towards strangers, more respondents trusted strangers they met face to face rather than those they encountered on line (*China Daily* 18/02/2013).

There are several elements to the trust needed in an information society: the reliability and value of the information that is available, the political colour of the analysis of it, the security of the data that is transmitted or stored, and personal privacy. The lack of reliability of information circulating through modern ICT platforms in China is a constant theme of leaders and commentators. One Chinese writer, Yu Hua (2012), painted a very grim picture: 'the country is now awash with supposition, half-credible news stories and libel against individuals, with the only real protected territory being the elite leaders and their lives. The rest of society is overwhelmed by rumors, campaigns and other material carried by social media.'

The problem of trust has been addressed by some Chinese scholars from the more general perspective. The conclusions from some of these studies allow us to conclude that lack of trust in the internet may be part of a broader lack of trust across the board in China. For example, one 2012 study concluded that 'Due to severe damage from the disappearance of trustworthiness, trust problems are multiplying in fields ranging from the economy, government, to culture' (Zeng 2010). The study cited data showing poor compliance rates with business contracts and high economic loss from fake goods. He said that the trust deficit would lead to a crisis in legitimacy for the government, undermine economic confidence in credit markets and result in a crisis in belief among the population. That study cites numerous social science surveys conducted in China with similar results.

But trust in the information sector was particularly damaged by the SARS crisis in 2002 and 2003 and has never fully recovered. One effect of this was to give an impulse to the idea of 'information ethics'. It is no coincidence that the sector in China in which this field is now most developed is the medical sector. Yet that interest in applying new ethics to information management has emerged across the board, with a clear surge in academic articles on the subject towards the end of the first decade of this century.

The turn to information ethics has been exemplified by increasing attention to the issue of privacy and its legal protection. The formal adoption of principles on privacy by the NPC Standing Committee in December 2012, already mentioned, followed more than a decade of planning and seven years of review. Typical of the calls for a new privacy standard was a proposal by one of the members to the 2012 NPC for information security to be developed as soon as possible, both to promote the development of modern information services and to protect the legitimate rights and interests of individuals, especially their individual security. That call was made by Xu Long, general manager of the Guangdong division of China Mobile (Ma 2012). On a similar theme, one Chinese researcher concluded that the situation of privacy protection in China is a 'fractured, episodic . . . patchwork of laws' (Wang Hao 2011). Wang observed that the 'understanding of the protection of privacy in China should lie in the understanding of what has not been done in Chinese legislation, rather than what has been done'.

The principles incorporated in the 2012 NPC Standing Committee resolution set out 'significant and far-reaching requirements applicable to the collection and processing of electronic personal information via the Internet' (Hunton & Williams LLP 2013a). By the time they were executed in the MIIT regulations of July 2013, the measures were seen as an effort to 'contemplate international data protection concepts' and 'an intention to import and apply these concepts in China' (Hunton &

Williams LLP 2013b). As that analysis discusses, personal information is defined as 'any information collected during the provision of telecommunications or Internet information services that would identify the user if used alone, or in combination with any other information'. The measures adopted in China follow a number of broad international standards on the collection and use of personal information, including 'obligations regarding notice, consent, collection limitations, use limitations, access and correction rights, fair and lawful collection, adopting security safeguards and notification in the event of a severe breach incident'. Penalties for violations in China's regulations include administrative warning, fines and, in some cases, criminal penalties.

On a parallel track, in February 2013, China's first national standard on data privacy came into force (Leu 2013), even if only in the form of guidelines. They defined personal information; made a distinction between sensitive and general personal information; and provided for consent for data retention, proper notification of purposes of the data collection, limits on international transfer, obligations to notify a breach, and provisions on retention and deletion. They are voluntary standards issued by the China Standardization Authority. To support the public release of the guidelines before they came into effect, the China Software Evaluation and Test Center (CSTC), part of the MIIT, announced in January 2013 that it would set up a multi-stakeholder group (government, business and standards centres) called the Personal Information Protection Alliance to serve as a consultative and self-regulatory body (Livingston 2013).

While promulgated in language that borrowed from international best practice, the philosophy behind the standards and measures was distinctly Chinese, or at least distinctly CCP. As one Chinese scholar observed with continuing relevance for today, the 'protection of privacy in contemporary China, compared with its past, has relatively increased consideration of personal benefits, but still takes social benefits as the centre of gravity' (Lü 2005). He said that the protection of personal privacy would continue to be limited by the 'social benefits and national interest'. He predicted some change to that balance: 'in public consciousness, the respect for privacy will become more widespread and more mature'. He saw quite some impact of international commitments, including by the WTO, on the evolution of privacy law in China. He foreshadowed that any convergence with international standards 'may particularly emphasize privacy protection consonant with more general Chinese ideas and values'.

In this situation, many of China's most creative citizens do not trust their more valuable communications to the internet or mobile communications platforms, nor do they trust Chinese government information on the internet and elsewhere. On the other hand, the majority of Chinese do. Within the political constraints they have imposed, China's leaders have shown an increasing commitment to building a secure and trusted environment for the non-political information ecosystem.

The test will come as China adapts to cloud computing, a global industry that stakes much more on trust and privacy than almost all other developments in application of IT technologies. The business model involves a decision by users to store or process client data in externally owned servers using externally owned software as a means of eliminating high capital costs and life-cycle costs for IT architecture. In 2013, as Chinese companies such as Alibaba and Huawei geared up to exploit the need for such services, and as global leaders in the field such as Amazon negotiated with Chinese cities and business partners to set up local affiliates, the Software Alliance (a group of globally prominent software businesses) ranked China quite poorly in its readiness and reliability for cloud computing (BSA 2013). On its annual scorecard, the Alliance ranked China nineteenth out of the twenty-four countries it surveyed, with a score of only half the best possible (51.5/100) and with especially low evaluations for privacy protection

(4.7/10), security regimes (2.8/10) and anti-crime environment (4.8/10). Only one of the countries in the twenty-four scored worse than China for security regimes, and none scored worse for anti-crime environment.

CONCLUSION

This chapter compared leadership values with the first set of three values listed in table 1.2 as ideal for an information society: freedom of information exchange, protection of such exchange by law, and promotion of trusted information.

Freedom of information exchange: The flood of information circulating in China had intensified as new forms of electronic media (such as the smart phone) and new platforms (such as Facebook or its lookalikes) came into being and found their place in China. There was visibly greater acceptance by the leaders that this was both natural and politically manageable. (Facebook was blocked beginning in 2009.) The major evolution in leadership values on FOI occurred in the emergence of the concept of e-democracy as a new form of citizens' supervision of the government and their society. This was portrayed by several leaders as a vindication of China's system of government, with a form of consultative democracy being held up as the right form for China. The leaders showed some commitment to open government and some acceptance of the principle of transparency in government, but these remained largely rhetorical in practice. There was a visible narrowing of the subjects that were considered state secrets, but it was only at the margins. By early 2014, as in 1999, state secrecy and state ideology were the dominant values in respect of information exchange.

Protection of information exchange: There has been a visible trend towards more respect for the rule of law by China's leaders than in

1999, but this has developed alongside an iron-fisted strengthening of their information control apparatus on a scale that matches the information explosion. China has now built the biggest and technically most advanced surveillance apparatus in human history, designed to prevent free exchange of information and to help punish people who breach government guidelines in information exchange. Throughout 2012 and 2013, advocates of greater protection in China of constitutional rights to freedom of speech became the special targets of a new crackdown. In 2013, as in 1999, arrests and imprisonment of journalists were stepped up, more liberal publications were closed, and issues from foreign news outlets were banned.

Trusted information: The leaders now place a much higher value on the reliability of research data and publicly circulating information than ever before. But their main motivation remains political, as defined by CCP needs and not by any inherent right to protection independently of that. The leaders have placed a much higher priority on the technical level of security of information networks, but China still lags significantly. The weak rule of law in China and political corruption affecting court cases together ensure that there are few protections for citizens. Moves by the leaders in 2012 and 2013 to protect privacy of information were weak and came after almost a decade of review.

What does this evolution of values after 1999 portend? Information exchange as a public value in China is alive and well (though with several important exceptions). Cross-border mobility associated with China's international exchanges in many areas (investment, trade, culture, education, military and political) has transformed the access of Chinese citizens to information beyond the control of the CCP. This is not a question of the internet as the main influence, but rather of globalization in all its dimensions.

China's political system has been irreversibly changed by the advent of a global information society, but there are clear exceptions to the unfettered flow of information. As MacKinnon (2011) observed and as this chapter confirms: 'Chinese authoritarianism has adapted to the Internet Age not merely through the deployment of Internet filtering, but also through the skilled use of second- and third-generation controls.' This is still an information dictatorship even if in political science terms it looks unlike any dictatorship that existed previously. In spite of the overwhelming pluralism of thought and information so visible in China, the CCP has been able to achieve what looks more or less like a steady state in terms of the secrecy of the government. One of the underpinnings of this appears to be a social contract that trades 'online activism' for 'offline obedience' (Herold 2013). Part of this contract is that 'Problems are to be defined as *social*, not as *political* problems, all problems are *local* in nature, not *national*, and the government is very responsive to citizen complaints' (Herold 2013 citing *China Youth Daily* 2009). China's leaders must be content with the fragmented authoritarianism that has emerged (Lieberthal and Oksenberg 1988; Benney 2013). They will be satisfied that even though media pluralism has contributed to the ability of citizens to confront the authorities and assert change, the citizen voice is also fragmented. The activism of lawyers around emerging lines of public protest, like 'rights defence' or constitutionalism, is unlikely to move the government from its path of fragmented authoritarianisms (Benney 2013).

As long as the Chinese leaders can marshal popular support through a mix of good policy, good propaganda and effective repression of opposition, they will continue to benefit from the information explosion. Zhao Yuezhi (2008) concluded that the leadership agenda of legitimation through e-democracy had benefited from the way in which the political economy of the communications system in the country had developed. He suggested that 'commodified media and popular culture', including watchdog journalism, popular television dramas and internet chat rooms, created a 'buffer zone for the party-state to redefine and reestablish hegemony over a deeply fractured and rapidly globalizing Chinese society'. Yet Zhao also concluded at the same time that 'the party's revolutionary legacy, its socialist pretensions, as well as popular demands for social justice and equality continue to feed into multifaceted elite and popular resistance' through the new media, and serve as a countervailing force against this legitimation of CCP governance by the same media. His assessment was that even though the Party had succeeded in 'capturing the commanding heights' of the political economy of new media, the effects had been to deepen the contradictions in the country. He talked of the pervasive conflict between the rulers, the capitalist class and its 'subaltern classes'. There is no single-minded party state, he says.

The underlying ethical stance of China's leaders on their information ecosystem is captured well by Xiao (2012) in his study on 'China's limited push model' of FOI. While pleading for recognition that at least there is an FOI debate in China and corresponding legislation, Xiao concludes that in spite of 'multiple paths for information flow', China's current official approach to FOI is undermined by several factors, 'including a limited access mechanism, broad and vague exemptions and omission of the maximum disclosure principle' present in some other countries' legislation.

The current state of China's information freedom (especially in academic and policy settings and in public) is at about the maximum it could be in a country that remains in practice a secret state governed by a secretive party. The constraints imposed by politics and ideology on freedom of information exchange, including through repression of individuals, are probably at their lowest since the Communists came to power. The focus of restrictions is probably at its narrowest as well. Yet, in their commitment to transparency, China's leaders have not yet equalled the commitment shown by Mikhail Gorbachev in the USSR beginning in 1987 with his policy of glasnost (meaning 'openness' or 'candour'), even though the volume and quality of information exchange in China today are massively greater than in the Soviet case. What this comparison highlights is that China's leaders, while still determined to repress certain forms of information exchange, could not be much closer to a tipping point in this area of policy if they tried, in spite of their own values. The quantity, frequency and speed of communications by ordinary citizens, specialist researchers, commercial interests and political activists in China and outside it are all now so great that information exchange seems like a political tsunami approaching China's political leaders with inexorable force to wash away the secret state. The publication globally of detailed information on the wealth of the immediate families of Xi Jinping and Wen Jiabao by Bloomberg and the *New York Times* was just a warning tremor of the character of the CCP's looming information catastrophe. The CCP could only survive such an event if it was itself able to construct a deeper consultative democracy and dilute its i-dictatorship.

4 | Innovative Information Economy

By 2000, the information technology sector represented around 33 per cent of the industrial output in Beijing, making it the largest industrial sector in the capital (Dai 2002). At the same time, China's output of information technology manufactures was growing at twice the speed of the rest of the economy, a growth rate that was itself high compared with the rest of the world. Young expatriates returning from the United States or Europe were responsible for setting up most of China's new high-tech companies (Meng and Li 2001). Investment from electronics enterprises in Taiwan, Japan and the United States was helping China make a good transition towards large-scale ICT exports. State ownership in the electronics sector had already been reduced to around 50 per cent (from 100 per cent twenty years previously). Against this background of success, Chinese leaders were by 2000 already very confident that within a decade or two the country would be a world power in the ICT sector in terms of manufacturing goods and providing related services. The leaders were less confident that they would be able to leverage the gains in manufacturing information technology products based on foreign inputs to help create an innovative information economy and society. They knew then that informatization of all sectors in a large developing country like China, with its political history and system, and at its stage of economic development, was going to take a long time. They set a horizon of 2050, a schedule that was neither that firm nor scientifically determined but rather intended to convey a long time in the future. There would be at least another five leadership generations in the Communist Party and government before then.

The new innovative economy ambition represented a quantum leap for China away from a policy setting of gradual economic reform carefully controlled by the government inside strictly managed borders. The new setting was one of fast-paced change, driven by industry and competitive trends outside China and by private capital, in which China's economy had to be fully internationalized and more heavily privatized. The leaders felt they had no choice. This was the character of the global economy in which China would rise or fall. They had to adapt or else fall behind (Jiang 2010; Qu 2010).

This chapter provides an overview of China's leadership values for an innovative information economy from the year 2000 onwards, that is, the second set of ideal values outlined in table 1.2. The chapter sketches how the leaders navigated this commitment at a policy level against their certain knowledge of the dilemmas they faced and the demands of the task. The first section looks at the leaders' commitment to the goal of transformation through innovation in informatization (information science, IT and information services). The second section traces the evolution of the leaders' approach to using informatization as a foundation of innovation. The third section looks at their commitment to developing the country's human resources, the creation of a class of information innovators on the one hand and, on the other, of the social environment in which information innovation is rewarded.

COMMITMENT TO TRANSFORMATION

To help make informatization a high national priority in 2000, the CCP leaders commissioned the World Bank to offer its advice. The response painted a grim picture: 'China's R&D effort is only 0.7% of GDP, which is low by international standards, and is barely 1% of global R&D. Its output in terms of international patenting is negligible.' It warned that China need to shift from its factor-based strategy (understood as industrial and agricultural production) to an information strategy based on knowledge production (World Bank 2000). A follow-on World Bank report one year later, negotiated between Chinese specialists and the Bank, offers some insight into how the Chinese leaders were framing their decisions (World Bank 2001). Its assessment was that the information revolution was exacerbating the country's other challenges in economic catch-up. The Bank advised that China would need to:

- update its economic and institutional regimes (especially the rule of law)
- upgrade education and learning
- build information infrastructure
- diffuse new technologies actively throughout the economy
- improve the research and development system
- exploit global knowledge.

The response from government was that informatization would be the 'key to our country's optimal industrialisation' (Qu 2010). The 10th Five-Year Plan (2001–5) was the first to include informatization as a strategic priority (one of sixteen such priorities). It set the following goals:

- raise the penetration rate of computers, improve access to computer networks and apply information technology as widely as possible
- use digital and network technologies as widely as possible
- complete the construction of the information infrastructure (national broadband network, increased use of the internet, and the convergence of the telecommunications networks, TV broadcasting networks and computer networks)
- promote the IT sector

- provide universal education in knowledge and skills for informatization. (Dai 2002)

There is a visible mismatch between, on the one hand, the expansive and transformative political character of the goals suggested in the 2001 World Bank report and, on the other, the priorities of the informatization strategy in the 2001–5 Plan. Thus, at the outset, the goal of transformation of the country into an information society took on a more technocratic bias that focused more on physical measures (manufacturing output, network development and throughput of students). In the balance between connectivity and content it was the former that was clear favourite. Some might argue that this was forced on the leaders by the realities of China and that the leaders acted wisely to sequence the technological development ahead of the social innovations that would eventually be necessary.

Throughout 2000, China undertook a number of other measures to kick-start the transformation, especially the reform of laws for venture capital, partial privatization of state-owned telecommunications utilities, introduction of domestic competition in telecommunications, and hosting of the first International Forum on City Informatization in the Asia Pacific. The breakthroughs in policy in 2000 owed a lot to the decision by China in 1999 to finalize negotiations with the United States on terms that would allow China to join the WTO (to which it acceded in 2001). But the consequential positive impacts of the WTO decision that benefited the information society ambition were not necessarily all intended (Mueller and Lovelock 2000).

Of special significance for the time is that China did not have a large corpus of people qualified in information technology. The count of students enrolled at tertiary level with information technology as a main subject or specialization numbered only in the thousands (in a population of one billion). By 2005, after years of expansion, the number was still just under 10,000. This meant that, at the outset, the revolutionary move to an ICT-based innovative economy was being driven by technology that was heavily dependent on foreigners, mostly Americans or American-owned companies, and paid for in US dollars at or near US prices.

Over the next several years, further policies complementary to the industrial transformation vision were introduced. One of the most important was the 2002 approval by the State Council of a suite of policies for setting up viable domestic industries in IT software and integrated circuits. The same year, the Ministry of Education published guidelines on popularizing IT education. The China Software Association (CSA) admitted Microsoft as its first foreign member. Also in 2002, as a further indicator of quite radical change, China Telecom was broken into two regional groups and it listed four regional networks on the stock exchanges in Hong Kong and New York.

In 2004, the leaders made something of a corrective to their technocratic and industry-based approach to the information society when the Central Committee of the CCP issued *Several Opinions on Strengthening the Exploitation and Development of Information Resources*, which subsequently came to be seen as the 'first important document in this field' (Qu 2010). It advocated that development of information resources should be led by market forces and be focused on specific applications (Zhi and Gao 2008).

The breakthroughs now began to be felt with much greater effect in the turnkey area of investment and economic liberalization. In respect of the latter, for example, by 2004, all provincial branches of China Mobile had been listed on capital markets inside China in a further partial privatization: 'more telecommunication services to more consumers . . . faster than any other time in history' (Zheng and Ward 2011). The private sector was forging ahead, with China's Lenovo acquiring IBM's personal computer business that year, thus marking one of the greatest milestones in China's informatization history.

E-commerce was the area with most success in these years. This was because it was least dependent on the government and was driven largely by foreign firms outside China and by foreign-invested firms in the country. In 2003, the Alibaba group (which had been doing business-to-business e-commerce since 1999) set up its eBay lookalike Taobao. From 2003 to 2005, the National Development and Reform Commission invested around RMB100 million (a tiny fraction of the net value of the trade) in 181 e-commerce projects to stimulate expansion (Qu 2010).

The financial services sector was one of the highlights of leadership success in informatization in the early part of the decade. In 2000, a number of agencies, led by the Ministry of Science and Technology and the PBoC, set up an intensive research project devised to create from the ground up a functioning world-class information and communications architecture for financial services. The project was needed because of the lack of concentration of the required skills inside the country. The project mobilized 2,000 elite specialists who developed 180 pilot projects and devised thirty standards (Qu 2010). The goals were to interconnect isolated systems, to set up a credit certification and security system, and to provide linked customer services for payment. By 2005, the PBoC and eight ministries and commissions released a Notice on Promoting the Bank Card Industry (Qu 2010). Internet banking with individual banks had begun in 1997 and was already widespread (Laforet 2009). Data centralization for banks began in 2001, and in 2004 the SILG pushed for emergency back-up data systems for banks, while a number of leading institutions set up such systems throughout 2005. The advent of these systems allowed for much better monitoring by the central government of the macro-economy.

In the politically sensitive sector of agriculture, the bulk of the government informatization effort to 2005 was in developing basic online information services for farmers and extending the telephone network to all villages. Even though a formal commitment to informatization of the sector had existed since 1994, little had been done beyond building a database or the commissioning of scientific research, and there was not even an agreed strategy in place (Liu 2012). In 2000, only 0.5 per cent of rural households had a computer and the majority of farmers had not been educated beyond middle school (Wang et al. 2009). In 2001, when Sichuan province (China's breadbasket) addressed informatization, it focused on telephone connections, fibre optic cable connections and an information service. For this service, the provincial authorities nominated the weather agency to develop the Rural Economic Information Network, something of a mismatch between need and capability (Liu 2012). At the national level, an online supply-and-demand reporting system for agricultural production was launched in 2002, and an integrated broadcasting system for information sharing on the national agriculture website was initiated (Qu 2010). In 2003, Guangdong province set up a special programme to bring computers to fifty-one of its more mountainous counties (Qiang et al. 2009). Food traceability in rural areas (for public health threats like mad cow disease) was launched in pilot mode in 2003 (Wang et al. 2009). A number of education and social initiatives for rural communities, such as distance learning and library services, were made available at around this time. The government's biggest push was to get connectivity and computers into the countryside. Chinese sources say that they can find no official policy document with the term 'agricultural informatization' in it before 2006 (Liu 2012). The focus was on social aspects of the rural areas rather than the improvement of agriculture as an economic sector.

The situation and the outcomes in the manufacturing sector were very different. The main evolution that occurred in these years was the transition from computer-assisted processes and machines used in the manufacturing process (in place for a decade or more) to the take-up of advanced automation processes for management. One of the path-breakers was Baosteel, the country's largest steel manufacturer, which in 2000 took its pre-existing information systems for produc-tion and marketing and incorporated them into an enterprise-wide network that also included equipment management, office automation and databases (Qu 2010). Even so, the penetration rate for office auto-mation in the manufacturing sector by 2005 was only 20 per cent of enterprises, though 70 per cent were using automated systems for facilities management.

By the middle of the decade, in the light of this patchy record of progress towards an information society, the leaders were ready to expand their vision of transformation through information innovation. They commissioned the drafting of the NIP 2006–20. In developing this strategy (which was drafted through the course of 2005) the leaders turned again to the World Bank, whose specialists participated in drafting the Chinese policy. A summary of the main policy lines for that NIP's fifteen-year strategy can be found in table 1.1. For the sake of comparing it with the policy priorities of five years earlier, the following points can be observed. In the new plan, there was a stronger sense of the transformative power of informatization. It could increase the ability of the authorities to 'rule and govern'. There would need to be a push forward on the 'construction of a system of laws relevant to informatisation'. Micro-administrative reforms in information policy were made both possible and desirable. Market forces had to be allowed into play. 'All of society' would 'develop and utilize information resources'. There was a new emphasis on 'constructing an information security safeguard system'. Thus by the time of release of the first fifteen-year informatization plan, the Chinese government was much more in step with the World Bank advice of five years earlier. In fact, it was this plan – only released in summary form to the world in 2006 – which marked a more comprehensive commitment by the leaders to the goal of transformation implied by the concept of an information society.

The 11th Five-Year Plan, put in place in 2006, placed considerable emphasis on speeding up the development of the internet, especially through building a next-generation internet protocol (IPv6); the integration of the networks of telecommunication, radio, television and the internet; and accelerating its commercial application. The breakthroughs in China's position in manufacturing and design began to gather pace. The leaders' commitment to transformation of the entire society by informatization was now more firmly in place, and this was buttressed by other processes of technological diffusion (such as the private sector market).

The formal establishment of the MIIT in 2008 has also proven to be an important landmark in leaders' efforts to achieve a more transformative effect from informatization policy. Yet even after the reform, it had most influence in promoting ICT industry development, not in fostering the bigger goal of an information economy that would see wealth accumulate around knowledge production and use.

In the second half of the decade, the technological and manufacturing breakthroughs continued to accumulate. For example, in 2009, China began to issue third-generation (3G) licences to mobile service suppliers for the first time and one of China's supercomputers became the fastest in the world (for a short while before losing the title back to Japan). But the leaders now began to turn their attention to hitherto quite neglected areas of informatization policy, especially the need for exploitation of information resources in sectors such as agriculture and education for social and economic benefit. This interest at government level was boosted (and facilitated) by the market-driven processes of diffusion of information and its associated technologies (such as continuing steep growth in the number of internet users and the introduction of new private sector online services). We can take these two sectors (agriculture and education) as test cases of the leaders' commitment after 2005 to transformation.

In agriculture, the NIP 2005–20 included provisions for improved network access for farmers, integration of agricultural information resources, and standardization of information services (market, science and technology, education and health care). It also provided measures for managing the flow of surplus rural labour. But the first big push came in 2007 when the Ministry of Agriculture put forward a more detailed policy, the Overall Framework for National Agriculture and Rural Informatization Construction, 2007–15. Its goals were to accelerate agricultural and rural information infrastructure; to integrate rural public services, to improve social management (internal security); and gradually to complete a sustainable development mechanism for agricultural and rural informatization (Qiang et al. 2009).

The results, however, have been disappointing. In quantitative terms, this is reflected in the rate of internet penetration (regular users as a percentage of the population) in rural areas reaching only 27 per cent by the end of 2012 (CNNIC 2013). By 2010, only 14 per cent of primary schools in rural areas had a local area network and an internet connection, compared with 64 per cent in urban areas (Zeng et al. 2012). The government was simply not spending enough money on school informatization in rural areas (37 per cent of the comparable per capita spend in urban areas). One study published in 2010 made a fairly critical evaluation of government efforts in rural informatization, describing it as 'disconnected, and sometimes sporadic' (Xia 2010).

In education, informatization fared somewhat better after 2005 than before, though it too has been something of a late starter (surprisingly). The National Education Informatization Plan (2011–20) was only launched several years into the overall national plan, and was even released in 2012, a year later than its announced start date. Even though a Leading Group had been set up in the Ministry of Education in 2002 to develop a general plan for overall education informatization, the main practical output was a policy on automation of management systems. It would be several years later that the policy objective really took hold. One reason was that the associated internal resources were being dedicated to a speeding up of distance learning after 2004. Yet the Organization Department of the Central Committee of the CCP had also launched its own pilot schemes on distance education in rural areas one year earlier. In 2007, the Organization Department issued an instruction on distance education of rural cadres – indicating a policy preference (or at least a competing priority) for informatizing Party rule ahead of people's education.

Thus, in practice, the two sectors (agriculture and education) demonstrate at best a mid-level commitment by the leaders after 2000 to transformation of the economy through informatization.

In May 2012, the State Council identified the 'construction of informatisation' as one of several areas that needed the highest attention in the interests of economic development. Within this sphere of policy, areas singled out for action included upgrading the broadband network; speeding up development of the next-generation internet; promoting the integration of telecom, internet and television networks; and raising the informatization level in enterprises, social sectors, e-government and rural areas (Xinhua 10/05/2012). In a speech by the retiring general secretary of the Communist Party, Hu Jintao, to the 18th Party Congress in November 2012, the leadership reaffirmed their desire to quicken the pace.

In this environment, the MIIT announced on 24 October 2013 a new national informatization plan to concentrate on delivering its effects in more rapid industrialization of the country. It echoed earlier strategies, since its plan was to enforce them. Guidance from MIIT two months earlier, in August 2013, had singled out these priorities:

- using IT to drive the restructuring and upgrading of business structures in industry

- exploiting emerging technologies such as e-commerce, the industrial cloud and big data
- using better IT solutions to save energy
- boosting the capability of small and mid-sized enterprises for the integration of industrialization and informatization
- driving innovations in e-commerce and logistics informatization
- promoting innovation and the integration of the internet to industrial applications
- stepped-up government investment
- new skills development
- much better information security.

China's intent on transformation is very high by international standards. The 2013 WEF NRI ranks China 22nd (out of 142 countries and territories) for the importance of ICT to the government's vision of the future, well ahead of other major industrial economies, including the United States at 44th (WEF and INSEAD 2013). No G8 country was ahead of China in this measure. (The same year, China was ranked much lower, at 58th, in terms of the overall NRI discussed in chapter 1.) There have been few areas of human social activity in China untouched by the informatization goal: it has affected government, business, technology, industry, education, trade, financial services, health services, professional services, diplomacy and military affairs. Each of these sectors has played a role in bottom-up and horizontal processes as well as being subject to the opportunities provided by top-down, government-led policy settings. At a popularizing level, typical of a Chinese Communist campaign, competitions exist at many levels: the top fifty informatized cities, launched in 2010 by the China Communications Industry Association; the One Hundred Outstanding Leaders award for the promotion of China's informatization, inaugurated by the China Information Industry Association; and cyber warfare competitions in PLA universities. There has definitely been a spirit of mobilization around the goal of informatization in all of its aspects.

The main test of transformation through informatization will, however, be the quality of information resources that are translated into information services. *China 2030*, a joint report with the World Bank, reflects the Chinese government's vision for a 'modern, harmonious, and creative high-income society' (World Bank and DRC 2012). It identified the quality of information resources as an important area of reform: 'Improved information and greater fiscal transparency at all levels of government would bring many benefits. These include greater efficiency, reduced corruption, and improved creditworthiness.' The report saw lack of adequate information about the job market as one of the reasons why tens of millions of farm families are 'trapped . . . in low-paying, low-productivity work'. It also reported 'informational friction' and lack of appropriate rules on information disclosure as serious obstacles to investment. It observed that China's fiscal relations between the central government and the provinces were not well documented, and that when they were audited the main objective of the auditors was to detect malfeasance rather than to analyse the effectiveness of the spending (through a performance audit).

INNOVATION SYSTEM AND INFORMATIZATION

What value did China's leaders give to informatization policy in their attempts to develop a national innovation system after the turn of the century?

As mentioned in chapter 2, some of the more significant changes in innovation policy undertaken by China only occurred in the decade before 2000, or even just one or two years before. The KIP initiative, piloted in 1998, showed very well the leaders' appreciation of a concept of innovation needed for the information society. It had to be one that advanced the basic sciences of information technology and communications, while exploiting existing information technologies to solve high-priority scientific challenges in other fields.

By the year 2000, China had started to race in its pursuit of industrial and scientific innovation, as numerous indicators revealed. R&D expenditure by large firms and the government had already taken an upward turn. China was second only to the United States and in front of Japan in number of S&T researchers; and more than forty foreign R&D labs had been established in China, most of them in the ICT sector (Fuller 2008; Hu 2008; Xue and Liang 2008). And China had committed itself to a sharp increase in research in nanotechnology, following a US lead, which meant that China would soon surpass all countries but the United States in spending in that field. Yet there was no well-developed concept of how informatization might be harnessed to the goal of innovation beyond dissemination of the technology in imitation of patterns seen in the West (Qu 2010). There had been little attention paid in China's R&D efforts to the linkages between informatization and enhanced development (innovation) of various industry and social sectors.

At this time, there were four clear locomotives of more advanced R&D for ICT inside China: the CAS, the laboratories of foreign firms, the emergence of venture capital, and the strengthening of IPR regimes.

First, as far as the CAS was concerned, although it represented only about 10 per cent of the S&T research body in total, the leaders assigned it the leading role in pushing through informatization of S&T research and R&D. The CAS (along with other government research institutes) rather than the universities received the overwhelming share of government R&D funding in the first half of the decade.

By the end of 2005, when the first phase of the KIP was concluded, there was a sharper appreciation of where information technology sat in the CAS priorities. It was one of four sectors of national strategic significance. The other three were outer space, advanced energy and nanotechnology. This set of priorities sat alongside another set of five in sustainable development: human health/medicine, industrial biotechnology, advanced sustainable agriculture, eco-environmental studies and marine science/resources (Suttmeier and Shi 2008).

Second, the laboratories or other R&D units of foreign firms were increasingly prominent players in China's ICT innovation after 2000. One Chinese-authored survey, which started in 2004 but was unable to find official data on the subject, concluded that there were 335 such R&D centres in all sectors in the middle of the decade, of which about 22 per cent were in the ICT sector (Xue and Liang 2008). By 2005, according to information collected over several years, foreign-invested R&D units in ICT were probably employing some 20,000 research staff in China (Fuller 2008). There was a mix of orientations for these R&D units, on a spectrum ranging from an exclusively China-based operational strategy (selling into China) to an exclusively international orientation (production for export).

The positive results of these activities for China's informatization strategy are reflected in a very rough way by the increase in numbers of patents granted. By the end of 2004, the number of utility patents granted by the United States Patent Treaty Office (USPTO) to foreign-invested firms in ICT in China had reached 606 (averaging 200 per year from 2002 to 2004, compared with only 9 in the year 1997). Of some note is that more than half had been granted to Hon Hai, and some 16 per cent to Inventec, both 'hybrid firms' with mixed Taiwanese and domestic investment (Fuller 2008). It is also worth noting that China was not remotely prominent by 2005 either in its share of Microsoft's utility patents granted in the United States (0.001 per cent) or in its share of the global number of utility patents granted in the United States (0.04 per cent) (Fuller 2008). The former statistic shows that the Microsoft R&D effort in China was not at the time outward oriented, while the latter statistic shows that by 2005 China's overall R&D effort was not penetrating internationally.

The situation with R&D among foreign-owned firms or foreign-invested firms operating in China contrasted strongly with the situation of domestically owned firms. While large absolute amounts were being spent by domestic firms on R&D, and the growth rate of that spending was higher than for government spending in that area, the share spent by private firms on R&D relationships with universities or government research institutes was actually shrinking, a point of concern at the time because that relationship was seen as vital to expanding China's R&D capability (Orcutt and Shen 2010).

Third, by 2005 venture capital was still in its infancy in China but was clearly having an impact. In interim regulations in 2001, and then with a revision and formula promulgation in 2003, China set in place a new legal regime for foreign venture capital. By 2005, according to data collected by Orcutt and Shen (2010) that they admit may not be complete, the investments by venture capital had increased by a factor of eight compared with 1999 to US$2 billion in 2005, for a cumulative total from 2000 to 2005 of US$8 bn.

Fourth, China took strenuous measures to strengthen its IPR regime. Action in this area of policy was robust and effective, and geared very heavily to international standards. By 2000, the country had joined most of the major international organizations and treaties governing IPR. In 2001 it made major revisions to several laws; its formal accession to WTO that year imposed new obligations on it to protect IPR. By 2005, China was operating a moderately effective system of patent protection that had a significant bearing on S&T development. That system was adversely affected by the institutional and social environment (political control of the courts, corruption, and weak investigative capability) but overall the legal regime was sound and prosecutions or civil disputes over IPR were common.

But by 2005, looking at these four drivers of innovation, the leaders were not happy. They concluded that the balance between foreign innovation in China and domestic innovation was inappropriate. They decided that indigenous innovation would be elevated to the same status to which Deng had raised the reform and opening-up policy in 1978. This decision worked itself into a number of policy documents connected with the 11th Five-Year Plan, especially the Medium and Long-Term Development Plan for Science and Technology 2006–20 (MLP). The MLP identified three lines of remedial action with a typically Chinese propaganda twist emphasizing the nationalist impulse: 'original innovation', 'integrated innovation' (fusing existing technologies in new ways) and 're-innovation' (some transformation of imported technologies) (National Research Council 2012). Many components of the fifteen-year plan were related to advanced information technology, including 'mega-engineering programs' to be focused on core electronic components, high-end generic chips, basic software, extra-large-scale integrated circuit manufacturing and techniques, and new-generation broadband wireless mobile telecommunications. The turn in innovation policy flowed through to informatization policy more broadly, with the SILG in 2006 adding a technology committee for the first time. It was in 2006 that the SILG approved the NIP 2006–20, which included important measures to promote R&D and innovation.

The MLP, however, had several weaknesses. A number of foreign governments and firms believed that the emphasis on indigenous innovation, and its resultant regulations, would breach China's commitments under the WTO. One study faulted it on two points (Serger and Breidne 2007). First, by highlighting the tension between domestic and foreign-funded innovation, the government was ignoring the need to maximize and publicize the beneficial spill-over effects of foreign-funded activity. Innovation, the authors said, went beyond what Chinese companies could make that was new, and involved the ability of companies, consumers and institutions to 'receive, absorb, and internalize knowledge as well as new ideas, products, and processes' regardless of their origin. Second, the government should complement its attention to natural sciences and technology-driven innovation with equal concentration on 'markets and consumers, organisational and process innovation, social capital, and (particularly) trust and institution-building'.

The government's broader vision for informatization came under equally strong criticism at the time, even from Chinese. An independent commentator included among China's weaknesses in the ICT sector the following factors that had at least as much to do with social and legal settings as with innovation policy more narrowly defined:

- lack of business executives with global vision
- inadequate enforcement of IPR protection law
- uncertainty arising from transition towards a market economy system
- excess administrative interference in business activities, affecting strategic decisions
- a regulatory system inadequate for a level playing field in supply of services. (Li 2006)

Key findings and recommendations from the 2007 World Bank study (Qiang 2007) were a little more strident:

- China needs to strike a different balance between government regulations and free market dynamics.
- China needs to fix its protections of IPR because the current situation gives domestic firms 'little incentive to invest in product development'.
- Digital media development is 'hindered by weak R&D, a shortage of developers, and tough restrictive regulations on digital content'.
- 'Stimulating innovation and supporting R&D are essential for the ICT industry to attract investment, maintain high growth, and become globally competitive'.

So, by the second half of the decade, it seemed that in spite of China's undoubted advances – including a doubling of financial support since 2003 for R&D, and the fact that SIPO invention patents granted to domestic firms had passed those of foreign firms for the first time in 2004 – the leaders wanted more and they were prepared to do more. The mood in 2007 was summarized by Liu Yandong, the state councillor responsible for S&T: 'The majority of the market is controlled by foreign companies, most core technology relies on imports, the situation is extremely grave as we are further pressured by developed countries who use blockades and technology controls – if we are not able to solve these problems we will forever be under the control of others.' In a 2008 article, the former general secretary of the CCP and former minister of the MEI, Jiang Zemin, was critical of 'lack of nerve and knowledge to innovate' and a 'lack of confidence' in China's ability to compete with and overtake the most developed countries (Jiang 2010).

In spite of the criticisms at home and abroad, one fundamental and far-reaching achievement of the MLP and subsidiary documents was recognition that the national innovation strategy had to be enterprise-led, not government-led, and that it had to be based on a new and intense relationship between industry and the research institutes and universities (Etzkowitz et al. 2007). This policy shift to recognizing enterprise leadership of innovation was reflected in the following years in significantly increased flows of funding from the private sector, including venture capital, to R&D in China. Yet the policy signal did not bring about a shift in the share of private sector expenditure on R&D going to universities, and the government had to increase its share (data in Orcutt and Shen 2010). The value of private sector funding for its own enterprise-based R&D more than doubled. Private sector R&D may have been significantly higher, but one major source of innovation (the universities) was not benefiting from that.

In economic policy, the government continued to apply tax incentives to foster innovation, while in science policy, the CAS continued to deepen institutional reform. In 2008, the CAS set up the General Group for Advancing e-Science Applications. Its functions were to link the CNNIC and institutes, to provide e-science advisory services, to help design e-science applications and to implement them. It was also intended to promote 'e-Science ideology' and international and domestic exchange in IT sciences. The intellectual property office, SIPO, released a strategy document through the State Council that was part IPR protection and part S&T target setting (SIPO 2008). It said that by 2020, 'China will become a country with a comparatively high level in terms of the creation, utilisation, protection and administration of IPRs.' It pushed the enterprise-led concept of a national innovation strategy: 'market entities are much better at the creation, utilization, protection and administration of IPRs.' It aimed to ensure that the 'quality and quantity of the self-reliant intellectual property are able to effectively support the effort to make China an innovative country'. The strategy set goals for the coming five years. China would 'rank among the advanced countries of the world in terms of the annual number of patents for inventions granted to the domestic applicants, while the number of overseas patent applications filed by Chinese applicants should greatly increase'.

A very big boost from the leadership came with a decision for stimulus spending in response to the global financial crisis of 2008. This included US$25 billion for indigenous innovation over several years, with about one sixth of the money flowing immediately for the first phase of work on three 'megaprojects' designated in the MLP: core electronic devices, semi-conductors and wireless broadband. The rest of the money was also used in short order to launch another five megaprojects (McGregor 2010). Throughout 2008 and 2009, China again revised its patent law and associated regulations, bringing them more tightly into line with international standards.

By 2009, the negative policy impacts of the emphasis on indigenous innovation were being felt. The establishment of preferential policies in government procurement for indigenous innovation was being increasingly criticized as a breach of China's WTO commitments (USCBC 2009). The government guidelines identified six industry categories, of which four were in information technology, and which would be subject to a certification process to receive the label of 'indigenous innovation'. Some thirty-four trade associations from the United States, Japan, Korea, Canada and Europe made a joint appeal to the Chinese government to delay implementation of the policies to allow for consultation on more transparent and competitive arrangements. The US government also raised the issue directly with the Chinese government.

But 2009 was to become a landmark year for S&T innovation policy, and for informatization policy in particular. The CAS published a mobilizing strategy document, *Technological Revolution and China's Future: Innovation 2050*, which was to serve as an overarching strategy at the same time as marking the launch of a series of subsequent sector-based reports also looking ahead to 2050. The report, which had involved some 300 CAS researchers and experts for more than a year, recommended that China prepare itself for a new revolution in S&T in the coming ten to twenty years in green energy, artificial intelligence, sustainable development, information networking systems, environmental preservation, space and ocean systems, and, most interestingly, national security and public security systems (CAS 2009). Work on seventeen 'roadmap reports' for 2050, including the one on information technology mentioned in chapter 1 (Li Guojie 2011), was launched at the same time.

The leaders launched yet another initiative intended to promote indigenous innovation further in 2010 under the rubric of strategic emerging industries – singling out high-tech strategic sectors such as information, biotechnology, medical, new energy, environment, marine and space. These sectors lined up more or less with the frontier technologies identified in the MLP and the 12th Five-Year Pan (2011–15), but next-generation information technology was one of just several high-priority industries (World Bank and DRC 2012).

At around that time, leading Chinese and foreign specialists were judging that the country remained an imitator of technical innovation, including in information technology, and had not provided the enabling environment to start to approach the pace of innovation in key competitor countries. This assessment is starkly visibly in the CAS *Roadmap to 2050* (Li Guojie 2011) on information technology. This report was written by Chinese researchers, specialists and officials from a wide range of stakeholder organizations. As a result, this informatization plan was probably the most comprehensive and authoritative of its kind in the world. Such a comprehensive plan for the development of information science and technology actually served to highlight the lack of attention in previous years to an overarching concept of just how China would join up all of the pieces of S&T policy to become an innovative information economy. In 2010, the ACSI had begun to promote such an overarching understanding more aggressively by launching a series of 'blue books' (annual academic research compendiums) on China's progress towards informatization. In 2011, the CAS joined in this effort with its own blue book, the first monograph on the state of informatization specifically for R&D in China.

Yet in spite of the leaders' best intentions and some notable successes, the time-frame for the transformation remained protracted. A 2012 study by Chinese authors of the patents being granted by SIPO in the ICT sector showed that from 2001 to 2011 foreign corporations were still prominent. It cited data from 2010, showing that eight of the top ten owners of SIPO-granted patents that year were foreign companies. The one consolation was that Huawei and ZTE were the top two in the list (Huang et al. 2012). There were many other studies with similar laments about the state of innovation in China in 2012.

A study of informatization in China's Shandong province concluded that while informatization had played a positive role in economic growth, the role of capital and labour was more prominent (Fu and Yan 2012).

There was no shortage of policy recommendations coming from academia and elsewhere on how to boost innovation. The most important step needed was for industry to take a leading position in invention patents in China, an area that was still dominated by the universities, operating independently of industry in the R&D stage (Huang et al. 2012). Other recommendations in this short study included the need for more internationally competitive collaboration by industry, for more investment, and for more foreign R&D centres to be set up in the country.

In a speech on 6 July 2012, China's president, Hu Jintao, called for a step change in China's innovation strategy. The leadership wanted more emphasis on high-quality education, on creating social incentives for creativity, and on deepening the mix of foreign creative enterprise inside China. The national media reported the speech and associated two-day conference as laying out a strategy to build China's 'scientific power'. Overall, the coordinated message was that in spite of its impressive gains, China was failing to keep up in industrial and scientific innovation. Its education system was not producing enough people to meet the demand and too many of China's most talented people were leaving the country.

The *China 2030* report (World Bank and DRC 2012), a jointly developed strategic concept, proposed innovation as one of six pillars of China's future economic strategy. The report advocated the following measures, which expose some of the challenges in the process of implementing the MLP. It called for:

- increasing the 'quality of research and development, rather than just quantity'

- 'increasing the technical and cognitive skills of university graduates and building a few world-class research universities with strong links to industry'
- fostering 'innovative cities' that bring together high-quality talent, knowledge networks, dynamic firms, and learning institutions, and allow them to interact without restriction
- increasing the availability of 'patient risk capital for startup private firms'
- encouraging 'Chinese firms to engage in product and process innovation not only through their own research and development but also by participating in global research and development networks'.

The *China 2030* report saw the private sector as a critical factor since 'innovation at the technology frontier is quite different in nature from simply catching up technologically'.

That said, if China wants to have caught up technologically with the most advanced countries in two or three decades, it must make additional tough policy decisions. *China 2030* identified the following critical policy factors: effective competition, the composition of the business sector and its strategic orientation; agile policymaking and robust regulation; skill development; R&D; national and international networking to promote innovation; and the nurturing of innovation. The simple formulation here should not distract from the overall thrust of the report, which foreshadowed the need for further significant political and social reform in China if these factors were to be put in place.

In the sixty-point reform agenda adopted by the Communist Party in November 2013 (Central Committee 2013), innovation was a particularly prominent theme, especially at point 13, 'Deepen science and technology reform.' The agenda for change in innovation policy was a long one that revealed not only leadership assessments of the current situation but also the strength of their commitment to areas of policy on which they were prepared to stake their reputation:

- 'smash' administrative dominance and departmental fragmentation
- establish mechanisms to encourage original creation and innovation
- give rein to the guiding functions of markets in the direction of R&D
- establish innovation mechanisms that coordinate industry, schools and research
- move forward with commercialization of applied technology R&D centres
- build a national innovation structure
- strengthen IPR use and protection
- perfect investment risk mechanisms and innovate commercial models
- establish innovation survey and appraisal systems.

INNOVATOR CLASS

By 2000, on one reading of the statistics, China was already producing larger numbers of professionals in most areas of science and technology than any other country except India. Yet, in terms of meeting the needs of such a large country, the education situation was still grim. China was spending around 2.5 per cent of GDP on education, a lower share than other major countries (Japan 3.6 per cent, the United States 5.2 per cent). In that year, China had only 2,206,000 students in regular higher education (three-year university and three-year specialized college courses) (Yang 2005). The participation rate in tertiary education of 11 per cent was one of the lowest for any major country. China recruited only 2,100 new PhD candidates (doctoral students) that year across all disciplines (Zha and Li 2011), of whom only twenty or thirty would have been in information technology. A World Bank analysis conducted at that time predicted that, on current trends, China would catch up to India only by 2015 in terms of gross enrolment ratio for tertiary education (World Bank 2001).

China's response was a radical one. It undertook one of the biggest expansions of tertiary education any country had seen for a long time, and this was particularly evident in information technology, with a raft of initiatives beginning in 2001. One of the most ambitious that year was the setting up of thirty-five pilot software colleges of national significance, a move described in China as a 'revolutionary attempt to achieve a great leap forward' for the software industry (Qu 2010). In 2002, a pilot was set up at Beijing University. The numbers were still small, though: about 300 graduates per year on average for the thirty-five colleges by 2006. Beginning in 2001, the Ministry of Education also began issuing approvals for universities and colleges to teach information security (forty-nine approvals) as well as electronic warfare technology and cryptography (eleven approvals).

In 2002, the CCP and State Council approved a three-year plan for talent development in science and technology. Beijing University established a College of Information Science and Technology, based on four existing departments. It also set up an off-campus School of Software and Micro-Electronics for working adults (Hayhoe and Zha 2011). One year later, the leaders convened an unprecedented joint conference between the CCP and the State Council to address talent development, with Hu Jintao noting that heightened international competition could be seen as a competition for human resources (Simon and Cao 2009).

In 2003, the CCP leadership set up a working group to develop talent, emphasizing that it, the Communist Party, not the State Council, had the lead role in this vitally important area of nation-building. By 2003, contrary to the World Bank estimate of just two years earlier,

China had surpassed India in its gross enrolment ration for tertiary education (Qiang 2007). It was in 2003, in its *China Science and Technology Indicators 2002*, that China applied for the first time an internationally recognized system for evaluating the development of its S&T talent pool (Simon and Cao 2009).

The situation with information-related education was, however, a clear exception, both in growing faster than the general expansion and in job opportunities. In 2003 and 2004, for example, among the top fifty-six categories of bachelor-level courses, computer software was the single most favoured specialization by a long shot. It was admitting, teaching and graduating more students in those two years than any other of the specializations. Of some note is that its closest competitor was English language, itself an enabler of the technology transfer that the Chinese leaders were looking for. Moreover within the fifty-six specializations, there were seven others that directly related to informatization, such as computer science, information systems and information engineering. Added together, the ICT sector was accounting for a staggering 20 per cent of all graduates in 2004 (see tables in Simon and Cao 2009). Within the engineering discipline, the single category of electrical and information engineering accounted for 50 per cent of students. The students were making a judgement about future career prospects.

Even so, the statistics most often used were not really compatible with those used in other countries. Gereffi et al. (2006) cited a McKinsey Institute country comparison of engineering graduates capable of competing in the global workforce. It found that the United States had produced three times as many as China in 2002–3 and 2003–4, but that China may have closed the gap marginally in the second of those years. It also noted that there was a mismatch between the high growth rate of graduates from technical schools and a decline in funding for such schools, and that this was suggestive of a deterioration in education quality.

The biggest policy turn probably took place around 2005 and 2006. In launching the MLP and its NIP 2006–20, both analysed earlier, the leaders made strong statements that the human capital needed to achieve the informatization ambition would be a major target of policy. They also made it clear that the brain drain of skilled workers out of China should be addressed as soon as possible. Even though the number of scientists and engineers involved in R&D more than doubled in the period 1999–2006 (from 531,000 to 1.222 million), this massive growth rate was only just keeping pace with that of the workforce.

In 2010, China released its first public survey of graduate education (commenced three years earlier). It showed clear successes. China had quadrupled the number of enrolments in PhD programmes across all disciplines compared with 1999, when the reforms started, and in the same period it had doubled the number of regular higher education institutions. International higher education opportunities had increased, with a doubling of Chinese students in the United States compared with 2000, and massively higher growth rates from a low base of Chinese student numbers in Germany, France, the UK, Japan, Korea, Australia and New Zealand. The bulk of the expansion was from privately funded students. Japan had become a close competitor of the United States in overall numbers of new tertiary students from China each year (data in Li Haizheng 2011).

According to a representative of the Higher Education Evaluation Centre in Beijing, the tertiary education scene at that time was characterized by a long list of political and policy challenges: global multipolarity, globalization, the revolution in science and technology, informatization, internationalization of education, intensified competition for talented professionals, 'increasing pressure from China's vast population, limited natural resources, deteriorating environment, and transformation of economic growth pattern', an incapacity of the education system to produce enough qualified people, new demand for education and a relative shortage in education resources, a 'conflict between the need to invigorate the education system and the institutional impediments to it' and a 'conflict between the expansion of education scale and its quality assurance and improvement' (Ji 2011). While some of these may be familiar elsewhere in the world, one essential limitation in China was that the solution was being addressed almost entirely by the government.

The education reforms did not address advanced information technologies as directly as they might have. Unfortunately, as mentioned earlier, it took China until 2010 to release a long-term vision of this. It then published an Outline of China's National Plan for Medium and Long-Term Education Reform and Development (2010–20). While this covered the entire spectrum from primary to tertiary, including advanced research, it provided an insight into official assessments of the quality of the education system, including science in general and informatization in particular. It set the strategic goals of rejuvenating the country through science and education, making the nation strong by relying on talents and professionals, running education to the satisfaction of the people, and building a rich resource of human talent. Even here, though, innovation remained only one of several guiding principles to be addressed, alongside national development, personal development, promoting equitable access across the country and improving quality. The education plan called for the national informatization strategy to include a section dedicated just to education. It recommended the popularization of computer terminals, the accelerated building of e-campuses, and a broadening of accesses to the internet, especially in rural schools. It called for the upgrading of CERNET and the China Education Satellite Broad Band Transmission Net, advocated standardization of basic benchmarks for education informatization, and proposed the establishment by 2020 of a nationwide online educational service network so as to promote modernization of teaching contents and methods. One inevitable implication of the education plan was that the system of education would remain standardized at the national level. At the tertiary level, the plan declared that 'no effort shall be spared to produce high-calibre professionals and top-notch innovators.'

For higher education, the plan also called for an improvement in the quality of PhD education, for a near doubling of the gross enrolment ratio in tertiary education to 40 per cent by 2020, and for several universities to 'come to the fore' in world reputation by that date, with one or two attaining world-class stature (Ji 2011). Most importantly, the plan called for a retreat by government from the universities, and for the assignment of responsibility for quality assurance to be passed to the stakeholders. The implementing strategies for executing the plan were yet to be developed. Only thirteen provinces or municipalities (out of thirty-one) had evaluation centres; all but four had fewer than thirty staff, and six had fewer than ten staff. The government set up a trilateral mechanism (China–Japan–Korea) to try to improve China's quality assurance for higher education.

One year later, in 2011, the country issued a specific education informatization plan that declared that the policy and institutions needed for effective application of information assets to education were not in place yet. It said that the informatization of education in China was an 'urgent and arduous task'. The goals included the building of a talent pool and innovative capacity that would allow the country to make its way in an environment of 'increasingly fierce' international competition. The plan also called for the promotion of public security needs, such as prevention of transfer of harmful material.

These developments were occurring at a time when Chinese higher education was in something of a crisis. Leading university appointments were controlled by political considerations and CCP committees inside the institutions. One tough assessment from a US source painted it in grim terms: 'Chinese scientists and scientific managers admit serious problems of research creativity, fraud and dishonesty, weak accountability for research expenditures, troubled institutional arrangements for managing the nation's scientific efforts, and a serious undersupply of highly qualified scientists and engineers' (Springut et al. 2011). It said that the education system was 'more geared to test-taking than cultivating creative thinking' that might enhance the innovation system.

Taking a broader view of the state of the innovation system in 2012, the *China 2030* report noted that in 'a ranking of 40 countries produced by the Chinese Academy of Science and Technology for Development (CASTED) China is in 21st place with a point score of 58 as against 100 for the U.S.' (World Bank and DRC 2012). It suggested that 'China's performance has improved since 2000, in knowledge creation (now in 33rd place – a five point improvement) and innovation performance has risen sharply to 9th place'. In other measures, such as efficiency, intensity and quality of research, 'China still lags behind the frontrunners – the U.S., Switzerland, Japan and Korea – it is seeking to match'. Citing a second (foreign) ranking of countries by innovativeness, which included measures of human capital, investment in R&D, numbers of scientific articles, entrepreneurship, IT, economic policy and economic performance, *China 2030* reported that China ranked 33rd but had shown the most impressive gains of any country between 1999 and 2009.

China 2030 mapped out the policy path needed to achieve the country's innovation objectives (increased effectiveness of its basic research and the development of high-tech industries), but it said that success in these would depend on 'the availability of a vast range of *technical skills* for research, design, fabrication, production, information and communication technology (ICT) support, and eventually marketing'. While remarking that by 2030 China would be producing more college graduates than the entire workforce of the United States, and that the quality of university training was improving rapidly, the report admitted that the 'quality of tertiary education more broadly is a matter of concern, and employers are experiencing a serious shortage of skills'. It proposed a number of measures to redress the problems:

- further accelerate governance reform in universities, giving them greater autonomy
- tighten ethical standards in research
- diversify funding sources
- appoint faculty that ensure high-quality, cross-disciplinary graduate and post-doctoral programmes
- develop innovative approaches to teaching and mentoring, especially in analytical skills
- set up well-staffed, specialized research institutes
- increase investment by the private sector and the government in improving the quality of human resources
- encourage more leading foreign universities to set up campuses in China jointly with domestic universities to impart modern governance standards, teaching methods and research management.

In addition to the raw numbers of talented people who graduate from or work in research centres in universities inside China, there are a number of environmental factors that have a huge influence on the human foundations of China's information economy. These include the international mobility of skilled workers and the recruitment preferences and opportunities of China-based corporations and government agencies in R&D.

The last decade has seen a revolution in the mobility of highly skilled international labour in and out of China. That mobility has many sources. There are aspects of it that promote the information society ambition and some that detract from it quite significantly.

On the positive side, China has – as a matter of deliberate policy – promoted the transfer of technology and skill by foreign specialists working in or visiting foreign-owned subsidiaries in China. Yet this has had an unintended effect of decreasing the competitiveness of local firms and pushing them to lower-end manufacturing (Zhang and Tao 2012). Another shortcoming was that people working in the foreign enterprises were not really given wide opportunities to create intellectual capital that was transferable.

The market forces in China are not helping with advanced skills development. In early 2013, the salary of a professor in engineering was no more than that of an assembly line worker in some factories – less than US$300 per month (Bradsher 2013). There are opportunities for professors to earn more, but the scramble to do so is not conducive to optimizing research outputs. The poor salary picture has to be understood against the environment of increasing student numbers and deteriorating staff–student ratios.

One the biggest problems China has faced is the flow of highly qualified Chinese to work abroad, either as entrepreneurs or as employees, after 1989. On the scale of this brain drain, a joint China–World Bank report of 2007 cited data from 2002 showing that of 600,000 students sent abroad in the previous thirty years to study, only 26 per cent returned (Qiang 2007). Tung (2008) cites a return rate of around 30 per cent. According to US immigration statistics, some 700,000 Chinese were given green card (permanent resident) status from 2002 to 2011 (DHS 2012). On average, some 10 per cent of total new green-card holders in 2011 from all countries were skilled workers. Thus, an estimated 70,000 skilled workers from China were offered a pathway to immigration into the United States in that ten-year period. In 2007, the stay rate in the United States of students from China who had received their PhD degree from a US university in 2002 was around 90 per cent (Finn 2010). Chinese students have had the highest stay rate of any foreign country group in the United States since 1990/1, when it overtook that of Indian students – just two years after the Tiananmen crackdown. Also of note is that the sectors with the highest stay rates for China have been engineering, computer science and physical science.

In his March 2012 Work Report to the NPC, the premier, Wen Jiabao, appealed for a more attractive social environment for innovators. He said China urgently needed 'high-level innovative and entrepreneurial personnel, talented young people', who were in short supply. He invoked the need to 'attract talented personnel from overseas' and argued for the creation of mechanism for giving 'incentives to talented personnel' inside China. Above all, he called on the country to 'create a favourable social environment for them to come to the fore in large numbers'. Yet the leaders are not winning the argument. A 2013 study of 164 science and engineering laboratories in the United States found that 25 per cent of the labs were led by Chinese-born people (Tanyildiz 2013). A significant number of Chinese specialists are flocking to top jobs outside the country.

It would be easy to say that the brain drain merely reflects opportunities for specialists to earn more money outside China, but the loss of talented people on a large scale is a strong indicator that China is not judged by these people to offer the social, economic, legal or political environment in which they would prefer to work. If China wants to keep these people, it will have to, as the World Bank said, 'adjust' the settings. China has implemented special incentives to bring skilled émigrés back to the country, and this has seen some success as salaries and social conditions in the country have improved. Yet the problem still remains.

An in-depth assessment of the dynamics involved in the internationalization process of Chinese universities published more than a decade ago appears to retain high relevance for both its findings and its prescriptions. It concluded that Chinese leaders had so totally instrumentalized international scientific collaboration in the interests of national economic advance that they had lost sight of how much more could be delivered by the process in terms of integrating China as a more powerful actor and partner in global knowledge creation (Yang 2002). The author saw the same shortcomings on the part of many of China's scientists and scientific institutions. Perhaps his most apt prescription for the future was the need for China to undertake genuine academic mobility, with free movement of scholars in fields apart from teaching English.

The Third Plenum reform agenda of 2013 gave the innovator pool considerable attention, recommending the following measures: 'reform selection and management systems for academics, optimize the structure of disciplines, raise the proportion of young and middle-aged talents, implement academics' retirement and pension systems'.

At the end of the day, for a creative class and innovative information society to prosper, the rewards for innovators have to be more than just financial and the environment has to be conducive to innovation. This has not been the case for most of the time since 2000. One insider characterization has been particularly revealing. Qu (2010), a former vice-minister of the MII, and one of the driving forces in China's informatization for twenty years, compared China unfavourably with the United States. She said the latter had become an innovative country because it is a country of immigrants and its culture is inclusive, a process that she said stimulated innovation. She asserted the centrality of ethics: 'values are the core of an innovative society' and 'institutions are the guarantee' of values. She described culture as the 'biggest factor affecting creative scientific and technological activities' and 'at the heart of creativity in research as well'. She said that culture 'provides the set of values . . . upon which a society or social group makes its rules, regulations and laws' and asserted that 'an innovative culture is an essential requirement of and driving force for informatisation'. In a sweeping condemnation of the state of ethics around the information society ambition in China, she gave it as her assessment that China has lagged behind because 'there have not been any new positive cultural factors to be incorporated; there has been no institutional framework to provide the relevant support; and the cultural environment has not induced and encouraged innovation'. She said that negative elements of traditional Chinese culture, such as the 'excessive caution, complacency, . . . established ways . . . , unwillingness to excel . . . feudal customs (such as "home tradition" and "valuing official rank")', are still pervasive. She then faulted the 'negative cultural features' of the planned economy: 'self-centred departmentalism, cliquishness, a lack of entrepreneurial spirit, and inaction and passiveness'.

Qu observed that among the 'core values' needed for modern technological innovation, some are indeed found in Chinese society. These include honesty, questioning, fairness, cooperation and openness. By contrast, she said, other core values needed for innovation such as 'marketing, competition, democracy, freedom, equality and reason are not widely accepted'. Qu has laid out a broad ethical sweep. She describes values that can be classed variously as personal, political, moral, institutional or cultural. She seems to be asserting that some element of each dimension is important.

CONCLUSION

In sum, we can describe the evolution of leadership values in promoting an innovative information economy after 1999 as follows.

Transformation intent: As China's successes in informatization of the economy mounted year on year, the leaders felt much firmer in their conviction that transformation was achievable and desirable. Yet a succession of domestic and international assessments have reminded them after each new policy that they would need to be even more daring in translating their ambition into concrete outcomes. The transformation intent of national informatization has not been implemented in key areas of the economy, such as agriculture, or in key areas of social development, such as education, as rapidly as a transformation vision might imply. Gradualism seems to remain a dominating value (or at least outcome) for the leaders. The biggest change through the last decade or so in leadership values has been their willingness to consider a progressive ramping up of liberalization in industry policy and faster development of information resources.

Innovation system: There has been a deepening appreciation within China's leadership of the character of innovation and of what needs to be done to promote it. Several turnkey decisions beginning in 2000 have been highlighted, including the promotion of a nascent software industry. By 2005, there was explicit recognition of the centrality of individual enterprises and the private sector in general as the locus of a national innovation system. But by 2013, the CCP was using language like 'smash administrative dominance' in reference to what still needed to be done in this area of policy to lift the heavy hand of the CCP from innovation. The leaders had shown a stronger commitment to rapid reform of some incentives and institutions, such as investment regimes, especially for venture capital, but a much weaker commitment to reforms in the relationship between university research and the private sector. The leaders came to accept the need for much more foreign expertise as a main driver, but they did so within more elaborate techno-nationalist constraints, especially through guidelines favouring indigenous innovation.

Innovator class: China's leaders can point to the large increase in graduates across the board, much higher participation rates in tertiary study, and spiralling output of scientific papers. They can also point to their information industry entrepreneurs, like Jack Ma, who turned Alibaba into a billion-dollar business group. They are now national heroes. But Jack Ma is a self-made man, whose successes came about in spite of the system. Domestic and foreign firms are fostering an active and large cohort of researchers, technicians and inventors operating in innovative

R&D. Yet the leaders have shown only a weak commitment to addressing the social environment for innovation. They only began to address the education system itself as one of the main determinants for creating a class of innovators in recent years, and they have not wanted to eliminate political interference and bureaucratism in universities. Students still study Marxism-Leninism, and main appointments are controlled by CCP committees. The economic and social incentives for innovators are still weak. Foreign expertise is still viewed too much as foreign rather than simply as expertise. There has been an intensifying lament by China's leaders that, in spite of clear successes in innovation, the country is not building a class of innovators with the depth needed for China to ascend as fast as it wants to in the global rankings of an innovation society.

Thus, in review, it seems that China's efforts to establish an innovative information economy bear out the conclusion that such an endeavour has to deal with 'complicated feedback mechanisms and interactive relations involving science, technology, learning, production, institutions, organisations, policy makers and demand' (Farina and Preissl 2000). China's leaders were strongest in their commitment to an innovative information economy in the new openness that they showed by agreeing in 1999 to terms to enter the WTO. Their decision around 2005 to recognize the individual enterprise as the primary locus of innovation was also a significant change of values for the leaders. They have been weaker in their ability to manage the complicated feedback mechanisms and interactive relations between the different foundational elements in setting up a national innovation system. They had a very burdensome socio-economic history to overcome. A command economy based on five-year plans and SOEs is almost by definition a low-innovation model.

More importantly, the leaders' persistent reliance on a nationalist vision of innovation may have been misplaced. Farina and Preissl (2000), citing research by others, have questioned the continuing relevance of national systems of innovation, preferring instead a view that sees globalization as so powerful as to suggest that a sectoral characterization, rather than a national one, may be more appropriate. They refer to research that focused on sectoral innovation systems as a 'more coherent subset' of national systems of innovation, 'where the boundaries of the systems are endogenous, emerging from the specific context of the sector', and where private firms are central, and more influential than the institutions (Breschi and Malerba 1997). Breznitz (2007) has concluded that the outcome of each state's development path for rapid innovation-based industrialization is a unique socio-industrial system, 'with different strengths, different weaknesses, and a different distribution of the fruits of success'. He also argued that the fragmentation brought on by globalization ensured that particular countries would become more narrowly specialized in certain subsectors rather than being able to develop broad-based mastery of and dominance across all advanced ICTs. This conclusion means that in a globalized information economy China should expect to excel only in a selected number of sectors under an international division of labour rather than aspire to comprehensive competitiveness in all sectors.

The leaders' faith in comprehensive nationwide and national-level informatization may also be misplaced. Breschi and Malerba (1997) cite research suggesting that while institutions are important to promote technological diffusion, they can also slow down the process of innovation; and that national institutions can also exacerbate disparities between regional systems of innovation within one country. This pattern is all too visible in the case of China. On the other hand, to their credit, the leaders have acted in line with the proposition that innovation can be particularly prominent in selected localities that are rich in social capital (Breschi and Malerba 1997). In the case of China, this has meant certain parts of the cities of Beijing and Shanghai, where innovation has clearly taken off.

It is the capacity of governments to adjust that is one of the main determinants of success in a national system of innovation: 'Politics matters', since it is the art of 'crafting and picking alternatives' (Breznitz 2007). According to that study, politics matters most in three areas: setting the balance between multinational corporations and the national actors, assessing and redressing market failures in research and development, and venture financing. These three areas of policy are among the most sensitive for China.

The discussion here suggests that China may be able to operate closer to the technological frontier in areas where elaborate state structures are not involved, where state secrecy is not an issue, where the private sector is leading, where there is foreign investment or foreign trade (international competitiveness), and where there is open international exchange of information.

In the face of unrelenting advance in high-tech industries by other leading economies, China is now signalling a more urgent need to shift away from its old growth model of re-export of imported or adapted foreign technologies towards a more competitive high-tech sector. Yet by 2020, China will have to quadruple its investments in R&D infrastructure and personnel if it is to get the results it wants. An even more tolerant attitude to foreign enterprises (corporations and universities) will have to be a key part of this strategy. Somewhat surprisingly, China's leaders now appear to be opening up a lot of new ground for foreign partnership, even leadership, in helping to create a new innovation system.

5 | Security in the Global Infosphere

The bombing of the Chinese embassy in Belgrade by the United States in 1999 and reports that the United States had used electronic attacks of some sort to manipulate the power grid in the city put China's leaders on notice that the future of its national security was in IW. As they looked around at the opportunities presented by the global information society in terms of high technology, new investment and trade, they began to understand that they would need to pay equal attention to the associated innovations in international security, especially in development of the armed forces and diplomacy. The need was aggravated by yet further deterioration in the political relationship with Taiwan as the pro-independence candidate, Chen Shui-bian, won the presidential election on 18 March 2000. This raised yet again China's military tensions with Taiwan and the latter's military supporter, the United States. Both were well ahead of China in information technologies and their military uses. But China's entire economic modernization strategy depended on continued good relations with both Taiwan and the United States, as well as key allies in Asia (Japan and South Korea) and in Europe (Germany). So for China, its national security in the broader sense of prosperous and secure economic and social development was dependent on its ability to contain and/or deal with the negative trends in the international security order around the geopolitics and military uses of information technologies.

This chapter discusses how legacy values in international security policy interacted with new demands arising from the information age and China's own information society ambition after 1999. The discussion tracks the third set of policy values towards the global information ecosystem identified in table 1.2: strategic stability, bridging military divides, and interdependent informatized security. In this area of policy, China's leaders had far less power and far less direct influence on the environment and on outcomes than in domestic affairs.

STRATEGIC STABILITY AND MILITARY POLICY

The idea of international strategic stability remained a central plank of Chinese policy after 2000. China's leaders wanted peace so that the country could maximize the gains from it for its own economic development, especially in informatization. Yet the idea of strategic stability was more an ideal than a clearly definable commodity. For example, at times China would rail against US military activities in East Asia as a threat to strategic stability. At other times, especially in private, Chinese leaders would admit that the US presence was an essential guarantee of such stability given the military stand-off on the Korean peninsula and given Japan's likely interest in acquiring nuclear weapons if the United States were to significantly reduce its military commitments in the region.

We have a very clear picture of Chinese leadership views of the relationship between informatization and China's view of strategic stability at the start of this century from the speeches of the CCP general secretary Jiang Zemin, who was in that post to 2002 and who was chairman of the CMC until 2005. In December 2000, he made a speech to the CMC asserting that China's ability to fight an informatized war was weak (Jiang 2010). A country, he said, now had to exercise and defend sovereignty over its information if it wanted to exercise sovereignty over its territorial waters and air space. Informatized war would become the main form of warfare. At the end of 2001, the CMC again considered what had now become the 'most far-reaching and profound' revolution in military affairs in human history. The deliberation at the meeting had been provoked by use of advanced informatized systems by the United States in the invasion of Afghanistan. The CMC concluded that more than half of the weapons used were informatized. Most importantly, the CMC noted the correlation between effective use of informatized systems and space-based assets, noting that the US military campaign depended on a network of some seventy satellites. For China, from that point on, the development of military space assets became an even higher priority. China had launched its first dedicated military communications satellite in January 2000, as part of a new command and control system, and issued its first white paper on space policy in 2000.

It was almost certainly in 2000 or 2001 that the CMC commissioned a review of the impact on China's security of the IW capabilities of other major powers. It was also probably in that year or around then that the CMC set up its own Leading Group on Informatization (mirroring the SILG) and its own Expert Advisory Committee for Military Informatization (to mirror the largely civilian ACSI). By 2002, the PLA had formulated a three-step plan. By 2010, they would 'lay a solid foundation for force informatisation and mechanisation', with the latter complete by 2020, but the former only in its initial stage (Lai 2010). By 2050, the informatization of all the services would be complete and China would have the ability to win an informatized war.

Jiang made a speech to the CMC in 2002 that almost certainly drew directly from the PLA report. He did not say it explicitly but, reading between the lines, Jiang was making very plain that China was out of its depth in terms of informatized war capability. He identified areas where the PLA would have to make major organizational reforms, especially the area of command and control and joint operations (the latter regarded in the United States as an essential component for maximizing combat exploitation of information war capability). He foreshadowed a gradual informatization of the PLA over fifty years, while saying that the first decade would determine the outcome of the later efforts. He emphasized the importance of innovation, futuristic thinking and thrift, observing that 'no matter how much we increase military spending, we will never be able to spend what the United States does'. He situated the drive for informatized military capability against the need to maintain a defensive posture in order to set the right scene for the country's international political struggles. Jiang also directly canvassed the need to cut the size of the armed forces from 2.5 million to bring them closer to the size of the US and Russian armed forces and to whittle down the unusually high proportion of administrative personnel.

At around this time, the phenomenon of patriotic hacking – already seen in China in the late 1990s – exploded with even greater force. Chinese hackers reacted to a number of events involving foreign countries by attacking their websites or other systems. The phenomenon has never gone away even though it has cyclical peaks depending on events. Triggers had included a wave of atrocities committed against ethnic-Chinese Indonesians in 1998 after the fall of the Suharto regime; the bombing by the United States of the Chinese embassy in Belgrade; a strident statement in 1999 by Taiwan's president, Li Teng-hui, about the island's sovereign status; a historians' conference in Japan in 2000 challenging the historical record on the Nanjing massacre; and the collision of a US Navy electronic warfare and intelligence collection aircraft with a PLA air force fighter in 2001 near Hainan (Hughes 2003). In some of these cases, especially the reaction to the Hainan aircraft collision and detention of US crew, the hacking was a two-way phenomenon involving the other country as well.

In 2003, the CMC promulgated a shift in PLA official doctrine from fighting a local war under high-tech conditions to fighting a local war under conditions of informatization. The changes run right through the 2004 white paper on China's national defence, with an entire section on speeding up informatization that had not appeared in previous white papers (released every two years). Each section in the 2004 white paper dedicated to a single service (the air force, the navy, the ground forces and the strategic missile forces) begins with the need to informatize the weapons and operations. One most important aspect of the policy shift in 2003 was the need for very rapid catch-up. Subsequent policy statements, especially the bi-annual defence white papers, carried this sense of urgency and an exhortation to an acceleration of effort.

According to anecdotal evidence, the 2003 decision to adopt an information war doctrine was accompanied by a surge in PLA-related cyber activities. One of the most famous cyber 'attacks' attributed to China, called Titan Rain, was launched. It operated successfully for several years as an intelligence collection operation against networks in the United States and among its allies in NATO. This operation was to set the scene for other governments to begin to see China's acquisition of cyber capability as destabilizing, even if its overall military capability in informatized warfare, apart from espionage, was still weak.

The reference to 'people's war' in connection with the informatized war strategy is especially significant at this time. It revealed China's intention, as with its ground forces, to maintain sizeable militia forces among the civilian population, trained in information technologies, for possible emergency mobilization in wartime. For informatized war, this has meant in practice that the PLA would actively recruit large numbers of civilian ICT specialists to serve in a stand-by role (not in active service) to conduct coordinated and possibly uncoordinated attacks on an adversary. This has led to reports that China is maintaining 'hacker armies', for which there is some considerable collateral. There is, however, little reliable information on just how far this militia building for information reserve troops has gone – how many there are and how well integrated into joint operations they may be. One consideration is that some attacks emanating from China might be from overenthusiastic militia hacking units rather than fully authorized by the PLA chain of command.

The PLA's informatization priorities may have received something of a competitor for policy attention when in 2004 the CMC approved 'new historic missions' for the PLA. These related to the broader dimensions of national security, especially at the domestic level. They were captured in a speech by the CCP general secretary, Hu Jintao, made to the CMC, his first as its new chairman. In that speech he set out the new missions of the PLA as follows:

- serve as a pillar of strength for consolidating the ruling position of the CCP
- guarantee the continuation of the strategic opportunity for national development
- support the safeguarding of national interests
- play a leading role in maintaining world peace and promoting common development.

These were interpreted by one analyst to indicate that China now had an 'interest frontier' that is different from 'the confines of its traditional territorial boundaries', and that the interests included those in cyberspace (Lai 2010). This was seen as representing a shift from traditional 'national sovereignty security' to 'national interest security', and from traditional territorial security to a wider conception of security in the country's politics, economy, science and technology, social life, culture, information, ideology and military. On the one hand, these new missions seemed to be pointing in the direction Jiang had flagged for developing IW capability. On the other hand, they also represented important countervailing influences that might put more emphasis on the civilian economy than on military operational preparations and army building for advanced information war. The insistence on maintaining the 'strategic opportunity for national development' may have been a corrective to those in the PLA advocating development of asymmetric capabilities in cyberspace to challenge US strategic superiority more quickly. In my view, with their heavy focus on loyalty to the CCP, and the need to serve national economic development and to preserve the domestic social order, the 'new historic missions' were not an evolution of the informatization doctrine, but rather a complete distraction from it.

Yet the CMC did continue with the informatization agenda, if somewhat slowly, approving only in 2006 the official training regulations for the new informatized war doctrine. According to Mulvenon (2008), citing PLA public sources, the new training policy had three planks: simulation, networking, and training at or from base. But the picture painted by Mulvenon is one of a gradual process of introducing fairly basic IT into the armed forces for training, not training for the conduct of combat operations involving IW. It was in the 2006 edition of an authoritative PLA air force manual that the first mention was made in air force doctrine of information operations as the initial phase of combat (Cliff et al. 2011).

China's military policy on informatization began to take on a new sophistication. In December 2006, Jiang raised in a public speech the need to create an 'information deterrent' to complement the country's nuclear deterrent. In the white paper published that year, the PLA mentioned the importance of defensive measures against information operations by other states. In a statement to the UN, China gave a very sharp view of the threat: 'the development and broad application of information technology have entailed unprecedented challenges to the security of individual States and of the international community as a whole' (UN Docs A/61/161, 18 July 2006). The statement went on to say that the problem arises on the one hand because of weakness in the basic information infrastructure and on the other because of the 'misuse of information technology'. The reference to the weak state of the infrastructure can be read as tacit acceptance that this was a common problem shared by all states.

China further deepened its commitment to military informatization in the 2006 white paper, asserting the centrality of IW not just in combat or war but in terms of the overall balance of power: 'Military competition based on informatization is intensifying.' The PLA would henceforth equate its national military readiness with how far it had improved its informatization. The CMC had decided to step up efforts to establish a 'joint operational command system, training system and support system' for fighting informatized wars. On the issue of the broader tasks of national defence, the CMC set as a goal the improvement of the 'capacity of economic mobilisation to meet the needs of defensive operations under conditions of informatisation'. The proportion of specialized information units in the militia would be raised.

The PLA was, then, in a position to deepen the application of ideas about IW and the application of informatized systems. A major change in 2007 was an explicit shift from a narrow view of informatized wars that focused on computers, networks and the transmission of code to a more comprehensive view that saw IW as involving the entire electromagnetic spectrum. This was reflected in brief in the 2008 white paper (released January 2009), which set a new mission in informatized wars of ensuring China's 'electromagnetic space security'. To this end, the PLA would henceforth spend a lot more effort on training its personnel for combat in complex electromagnetic environments. This white paper summarized some of the other achievements across all military areas, including strategy, training and education.

Informatization was becoming entrenched in PLA consciousness. The 2010 white paper said that the advance towards informatization of society was 'irreversible'. That year, the General Staff Department (GSD) set up its new 'Information Warfare Base', for ensuring defence against enemy information operations and security of its own networks. By 2011, the PLA had consolidated a doctrine of integrated network warfare: 'the use of electronic warfare, computer network operations, and kinetic strikes to disrupt battlefield information systems' especially through joint operations (DoD 2011). Also in 2011, the GS Headquarters transformed its Communications Department into an Informatization Department, and ordered the establishment of parallel units in subordinate commands. The move was intended to improve the 'leadership and management system of the information-based construction of the PLA', according to the military newspaper *Liberation Army Daily* (01/07/2011). The PLA reported at the time that it had set up a team of thirty top-line professionals from within its ranks to serve as the blue force (the enemy) in cyber war games. By that time, the Guangdong Military Region (opposite Hong Kong) had established itself as something of a training base and testing field for PLA informatization.

For the PLA, IW was now becoming an operational priority, and not just a broad strategic goal. The 2012 and 2013 assessments from the Pentagon of China's military development observed that it was acquiring cyberspace capabilities 'that appear designed to enable' anti-access/area-denial missions (DoD 2012, 2013). China was seeking the 'ability to control and dominate the information spectrum in all dimensions of the modern battlespace' for a Taiwan scenario (DoD 2013). This report concluded that beyond the immediate needs of Taiwan-related scenarios, China was investing in programmes in areas like electronic warfare designed to give it a broader cyber military capability. The 2012 report paid some attention to the investment in espionage capabilities and their persistent use against US targets. The 2013 report noted important progress in command and control: 'Commanders can now issue orders to multiple units at the same time while on the move, and units can rapidly adjust their actions through the use of digital databases and command automation tools.' It went on to say that 'to fully implement informatized command and control, the PLA will need to overcome a shortage of trained personnel and its culture of centralized, micro-managed command'. This might be interpreted to mean that the PLA has automated the basic C2 systems (command and control) while aiming to master the most advanced C4ISTAR capabilities (command, control, communications, computers, intelligence, surveillance, target acquisition, reconnaissance).

In a 2013 press briefing on the annual defence budget, the PLA spokesman said the main priorities in this budget in the military technical area were 'improving the information-based equipment, strengthening the construction of the human resources and raising the informatisation level', alongside strengthening the joint training and joint operations of China's services (Wang 2012). In June 2013, the PLA conducted its first joint exercise using digital technology in a modern warfare scenario to simulate 'non-contact assaults' alongside conventional operations. The term 'non-contact assaults' referred to 'digital operations, including cyberwarfare, electronic warfare and intelligence warfare systems, as well as others'. The exercise, involving a group army from the Beijing Military Region, eight military academies and an air force school specializing in early warning, was probably intended to test out new joint force concepts. It was described by the GSD as China's first exercise in joint operations between IW units, electronic counter-measures units, special operations forces and army aviation units (*South China Morning Post* 30/05/2013).

In the sixty-point reform plan approved at the Third Plenum of the Communist Party in November 2013, the short sections on national defence in three of the points reiterated earlier themes relevant to informatization: joint operations, new leadership skills, unified management of informatized construction, optimization of the scale and structure of the military (i.e. cut numbers in favour of technology), better human resource policy systems, and a better national defence science and technology innovation system.

There have been at least three important exceptions to the generally slow-paced development of the PLA in military cyber capability between 2003 and 2013: development of space assets to underpin advanced C4ISTAR; cyber espionage; and development of one-off offensive cyber weapons.

The first of these exceptions, the space programme, has itself been a showcase of China's application of advanced information technology for military purposes as well as an underpinning of future IW capability. Though there are important civilian elements to China's space programme, the military impulse after 1999 has been significantly enhanced. Highlights of the programme include the successful ground test of an anti-satellite weapon in 2000, the country's first manned space flight in 2003, its first successful test of an anti-satellite weapon in 2007 in space (attracting massive international criticism for irresponsibly creating large amounts of space junk), and a soft moon landing and deployment of a lunar rover in December 2013. The programme has been a locus of contest with the United States, with the latter lurching from sanctions over missile technologies in 2000 to some bans on scientist-to-scientist contacts for leading US space scientists in two government agencies, including NASA, beginning in 2011.

The second important exception has been the high performance of certain aspects of China's cyber espionage. Its achievements against the United States have been well documented (MANDIANT 2013; Krekel et al. 2012; ONCIX 2011). In sum, they paint a picture of the successful exfiltration of large amounts of sensitive military-related information, as well as commercially and politically sensitive information. In respect of military information, the PLA places considerable emphasis on mapping the networks of potential adversaries (Krepinevich 2012). In respect of technology secrets, these successes have been labelled by prominent Americans as the largest illicit transfer of wealth in human history. China concentrates its foreign military intelligence on S&T collection and on US, Taiwanese, Korean, Indian and Russia military activities and war-fighting capabilities (including infrastructure). Given these high priorities, China may not devote as many resources to analysing all of the stolen commercial secrets as some US critics suggest.

One consideration in assessing China's military espionage capability is that a third party is able to misrepresent the identity of the attacker through a technique called 'spoofing'. This technique leaves open some room for third parties located outside China to be controlling the computers located in China to which an attack or malicious activity has been traced (Lewis 2005). Yet by 2013, a number of professionals in the field in the United States believed that the technical community outside China had made sufficient progress in attribution techniques, including through applying collateral information beyond the data available in a cyber attack software set, to attribute a range of attacks confidently to China (MANDIANT 2013). It appears that by 2013 the US government had relatively high confidence in attribution to Chinese agencies or semi-official actors of large-scale and highly effective cyber espionage.

It would only be normal for China to be engaged in such practices for national security reasons. For example, in all major Chinese organizations operating both in China and abroad – whether governmental, corporate or non-governmental – there would be staff in leadership and line positions who are in touch with Chinese intelligence services and providing significant information. This may be happening on a scale that dwarfs similar relationships held by US and allied agencies with their compatriots. According to a former director of both the CIA and NSA, Mike Hayden, we can assume that the United States had hard evidence that leading telecoms equipment supplier Huawei had spied for China (transcript of interview, *Australian Financial Review* 19/07/2013). Of note was Hayden's remark that the chair of Huawei is a former official of China's main foreign spy agency, the MSS. Another source for concern quoted by critics is that the founder of Huawei, Ren Zhengfei, used to be a member of the Chinese armed forces. (Ironically, according to one source, he was denied Communist

Party membership because of the Kuomintang political background of his parents. And he was pushed out of the army in the first big wave of demobilizations under Deng Xiaoping in 1982.) Huawei has strenuously denied the allegations about its spying for China.

The third exception to the generally poor development of PLA military cyber capability appears to have been in the area of testing offensive cyber weapons inside the critical military and civilian infrastructure of likely military adversaries (such as Taiwan, the United States and Japan). There is only scant information on this in the public domain. The most direct comes from a former official of the US National Security Council, Richard Clarke. In a co-authored book, he reported that China was planting 'logic bombs' in the US power grid that could be activated in times of tension or war to disrupt power deliveries on a militarily and politically significant scale (Clarke and Knake 2010). (The book says that the United States is 'presumably' authorizing similar operations.) Logic bombs could also be used to disrupt other critical infrastructure, including through the destruction of large amounts of data (Krepinevich 2012). On 13 February 2013, without naming China but alluding to it, US President Obama said that 'our enemies are also seeking the ability to sabotage our power grid, our financial institutions, and our air traffic control systems'. There have been sustained reports of computers traced to China undertaking such activities.

Thus, over the decade since 2003, China's leaders had come to accept that informatization represents a fundamental transformation in military affairs, that it affects concepts of deterrence, and that winning an informatized war has to be the main objective of military strategy. The PLA had also learned that information operations involving possible adversaries are ever-present, occurring every minute of every day. This has been a fundamental paradigm shift for an army that had until then been as much concerned with nation-building and political tasks as with preparing for possible war through occasional military exercises.

In an operational military sense, China's leaders have been slow to adjust in terms of fully embracing military strategies and operational practices for warfare in the information age. Most notably, there appears to be a mismatch between the very high priority placed on development of cyber espionage capabilities (to find out the cyber war capabilities and plans of its enemies) and the lower priority attached to informatization across the PLA. The intelligence task was urgent, while the informatization plan had a 2050 time horizon, or 2020, depending on how we read the relevant official statements. In an institutional sense, since China's political system favoured the rapid development of internal surveillance capabilities, it was only natural that the armed forces would develop similar capabilities for international espionage at a faster rate than for other IW capabilities for combat operations in a joint force environment.

It will be apparent from this analysis that public sources on the focus and plans for building China's military informatization provide only fairly general information. There are occasional gems in the Chinese military press. One of the more important sources of detail has been Western official assessments, not least the Pentagon's annual report on military developments in China and other intelligence assessments released to the public domain. These reports may overstate some of the developing capabilities but they nonetheless give an insight into China's priorities. There are numerous official Chinese sources that offer an assessment of China's cyber military power at a broad level. The more authoritative statements declare that China lags badly behind the United States (and/or its alliances) both in preparing the armed forces for war in the information age and in its ability to compete strategically in this age. For example, a commentary in *Liberation Army Daily* of 1 January 2008 saw the primary policy challenge for China as overcoming this deficit: 'the main contradiction in our army building is still that the level of our modernization is incompatible with the demands of winning a partial war under informatization conditions, and our military capability is incompatible with the demands of carrying out the army's historic missions in the new century and new stage' (cited in Mulvenon 2009). The 2010 white paper on national defence, published in 2011, reported that while the PLA had advanced in informatization infrastructure, it had obtained only a 'preliminary level' of 'interoperability between different elements of its armed forces within this sphere' (i.e. informatization). China's assessment has consistently been that the 'United States has established the leading position in the military realm' of the information age because of its overall scientific and technological lead (Qu 2010). Echoing this assessment, a Chinese military observer writing in 2012 commented that 'all core technologies are basically in the hands of U.S. companies, and this provides perfect conditions for the U.S. military to carry out cyber warfare and cyber deterrence' (see Segal 2012, citing the military newspaper *China Defense.*) Moreover, the United States maintains a restriction on exports of high-tech equipment to China under numerous legislative regimes, in areas such as chemical and biological weapons precursors, nuclear non-proliferation, national security, missile technology, regional stability and firearms.

Authoritative Western sources agree that China has made slow progress. Polpetter (2010) observed that between 1999 and 2009, the PLA had made 'only desultory progress' in moving to joint operations and was therefore unable to win informatized wars. Scobell (2010) concluded that the 'overall level of information technology employed across the PLA is low and rudimentary despite pockets of high-tech information technology (IT) sophistry'. Ball (2011) assessed that China's military leaders must be in a state of 'despair at the breadth and depth of modern digital information and communications systems and technical expertise available to their adversaries'. He concluded that 'China is condemned to inferiority in IW capabilities for probably several decades'. Hjortdal (2011) offers a balanced summary of the main considerations, touching in passing on China's sense of insecurity in the military cyber domain and how the need to catch up could be driving its plans.

Such negative assessments can be contrasted with others that seem more positive. For example, Clarke and Knake (2010) concluded that even though China's capability for offensive cyber operations is markedly weaker than that of the United States, its overall capability for what they call 'cyber war' may be superior because China has advantages in cyber defence and because its level of dependence on cyber systems is lower. There is some anecdotal evidence that in certain scenarios that have been war-gamed in the United States, an adversary like China could gain the strategic advantage through advantageous use of information weapons and related operations. The value of such anecdotal evidence is not in proving one way or the other which country of the two may have, in some static sense, a superior order of battle for cyber war, but rather in reminding us that the best measure of military preparedness and strategic capability will be one that takes account of the dynamic environment and human decision-making. It is in these areas that both Chinese and Western sources find agreement. China is weaker by far for most scenarios of sustained military combat 'under informatised conditions' than the US global alliance or simply the US alliance power in East Asia (including Japan, Taiwan, South Korea and Australia).

China's cyber espionage has been seriously destabilizing, most conspicuously in China's relations with the United States (discussed further in the following sections). By the time Edward Snowden, beginning in June 2013, leaked classified documents on US and allied cyber espionage, the global infosphere was anything but stable. In a unique joint study between Chinese and Americans published by EastWest in November 2013, the number one concern raised by the Chinese participants was militarization of the internet and the cyber arms race (Rauscher and Zhou 2013). There is clearly an arms race in cyberspace that China's leaders feel they are losing. They have been showing few signs that they intend to take a unilateral lead to stabilize the situation.

BRIDGING MILITARY DIVIDES

Chapter 1 identified how in practical policy terms China's ambition for the information society is hamstrung by the strategic divide between the 'two camps', the other camp being the community of liberal pluralist, capitalist countries. Chapter 4 showed how in the case of investment and trade, the significance of the two-camps division has been massively eroded. In spite of that, there are two sets of circumstances that contribute to its persistence.

The first of the circumstances defining the 'two-camps divide' today and since 1949 has been Taiwan. That year, the Nationalist forces (the ROC government) were finally defeated in the Civil War on the mainland and, as a last refuge, fled to the island of Taiwan, which had been in Japanese hands between 1895 and 1945. Since 1979, when the United States finally withdrew diplomatic recognition from the ROC in favour of the PRC, China has actively espoused a policy of peaceful reunification but reserves the right (since it sees Taiwan as national territory and part of its sovereignty) to 'protect it' from breaking away through use of armed force if necessary. For this reason, the United States made a commitment in 1979 through the Taiwan Relations Act passed by its Congress to provide for the defence of Taiwan.

In January 1995, China made a major change in its policy on this issue by citing the principle that 'Chinese should not fight Chinese.' At the same time it maintained that 'We do not promise not to use force.' When an eight-point plan put forward with these statements was rebuffed by Taiwan later that year, and after the US government was forced into a humiliating back-down by its own Congress to permit a visit by Taiwan's leader, Lee Teng-hui, China resorted to military threats. These included the unprecedented launch in July 1995 and

March 1996 of small numbers of medium-range ballistic missiles over Taiwan. The splash-down areas in the sea were so close to Taiwan that the intent to threaten it and warn off the United States from military intervention was unmistakable. China's build-up of missile capability opposite Taiwan since then has exacerbated the two-camps divide between it and Taiwan on the one hand, and between China and the United States (and its allies) on the other. In its public ethics on Taiwan, China sees itself as very much in the right and adopting a defensive position even if that puts at risk its access to Taiwanese and US investment and capital for China's informatization.

The nature of the division between Taiwan and China changed radically in the decade beginning 2000 – from one of sharp confrontation, one-way investment and one-way people movement to a relationship of mutual exchange, large-scale, two-way people movement through direct transport links, and reduced political tensions. While political relations remained difficult while the pro-independence president Chen Shui-bian was in office (until 2008), economic relations continued to deepen. The military stand-off between the two was never far from public view. In 2008, the Guomindang (Nationalist Party) regained power. It had ruled China before its defeat on the mainland in 1949, and Taiwan continuously from 1945. Better known in English by the initials KMT, it has presided since 2008 over a significant warming of relations with China. This included a return in that year to high-level contacts suspended since 1999; a lifting of the remaining bans on certain types of investment in China; and the restoration of direct flights, post and trade that had been suspended for more than fifty years.

The deepening of China–Taiwan relations accelerated. By the end of 2012, China (including Hong Kong) was taking 40 per cent of Taiwan's trade, with the United States dropping to a 10 per cent share (Meltzer 2013). This represented a reversal over two decades of the relative positions of China and the United States in Taiwan's trade pattern. It is an historic evolution, even if, as Meltzer points out, the United States is a primary destination of production from Taiwan-invested factories in China. By 2013, Zeng Peiyang, a former Politburo member and champion of the ICT sector, made an official visit to Taiwan for an industrial and economic inspection tour, a sign of his continuing interest in the informatization goal and the leadership's acceptance of Taiwan's likely future role in that. By October 2013, a vice-minister from China's MIIT was in Taiwan inviting joint research and development on 5G mobile technology. On National Day on 10 October 2013, KMT President Ma signalled further political breakthroughs when he made two statements that together strengthened his government's commitment to the principle of one China: he said that cross-strait relations are not 'international' in character and that Taiwanese are part of the Chinese ethnicity. China has not abandoned its military preparations for Taiwan contingencies, and the government of Taiwan remains suspicious of China and alert to possible military moves, but there has been a sea change in relations since 2000. This was demonstrated in the first official meeting between government representatives of the two sides since 1949. It was held in Nanjing, China, on 11 February 2014, and the two sides agreed to hold further meetings.

Second, the two-camps divide has not just been about the prospects for military conflict between China and Taiwan. It came about in the first instance, and it persists, because of the differences in ethical values about political governance between China on the one hand and the United States and its closest political allies on the other. The latter camp supports a multi-party political system with separation of powers and the rule of law, while China supports a one-party political system with no effective separation between the judicial, legislative and executive bodies on matters of high policy. As the case of continuing tensions between Russia and Western countries on such issues demonstrates, even though Russia has a multi-party system, the differences over the ethics of the political system undermine strategic trust, regardless of the actual military strategic orientation of the armed forces of the two countries. For strategic decision-makers on either side of China's two camps, the other side is simply 'untrustworthy'. The ethical values of the two sides on this set of issues are not mirror images. China is simply and viscerally opposed to the sustained interference by the other camp in its internal political affairs, seen by China as breaching the principle of non-interference embodied in the UN Charter. The other camp – the US-led Western alliance – sees itself as the defender of human rights in countries such as China, which it faults robustly almost on a daily basis. The sense of moral outrage that Chinese leaders, including especially its military leadership, feel on this subject – seeing the actions as invasive of both dignity and territory – is argu-ably far stronger than the sense of moral outrage felt by those govern-ments that intervene with China on human rights issues. China's response on these issues has not changed for decades. It consists of rejecting such criticisms out of hand while doing its best to ensure that disputes on such issues have as little impact as possible on continued Western investment and trade in China's advancing information economy. At the same time, China has shown a softening on certain issues, and shifted its ethical stance on important human rights issues, including through a public commitment to ban torture and root it out of the legal system.

Ever since China's leaders adopted the information society ambition in 2000, they have railed against the digital divide at the international level. Sometimes they emphasize the wealth gap between developed and developing countries as the main characteristic. They see the lack of resources in developing countries as the main explanation for lack of diffusion of advanced information technologies and for the existence of the digital divide. On other occasions, the leaders see the great power mentality of the United States and its allies as the main cause of the digital divide, and more importantly as the main cause of insecurity – because the US global military alliance has a commanding position in global ICT resources, especially advanced technologies. But there is a third characterization that is also raised by the Chinese leaders that affects national security. They say that the divide is in fact contrary to the interests of all parties because it does not recognize the fundamentally deep level of interdependence of cyberspace, even in terms of national security. Moreover, it interferes with the international community's ability to apply advanced ICTs jointly to solving some of the major global security challenges.

China and the United States both have a strong interest in cooperating on certain aspects of cyber security arising from their mutual economic interdependence (Inkster 2010). Trillions of dollars of transactions occur through digitally networked communications each day. In speaking of the US economic reliance on digital networks and systems, a former director of national intelligence, Mike McConnell, observed in 2010: 'If those who wish us ill, if someone with a different world view was successful in attacking that information and destroying the data, it could have a devastating impact, not only on the nation, but the globe' (Intelligence Squared Debate 2010).

The likely costs to global economic stability of a major confrontation between China and the United States that affected these digital systems, or confidence in these systems, would be very high. The threat of distributed denial of service attacks – delaying transactions or market access, deleting databases and transactions – would have major negative repercussions for the global economy and plunge large parts of the world into recession (Tendulkar 2013). Whether confidence after such an attack could be restored remains an open question. These costs would be so high that they should deter dependent states from attacking these information systems or their infrastructure to solve political conflict. Cyberspace only amplifies traditional interdependence in trade.

At a lower level of interdependence, China's high reliance on foreign manufacturing investors for its 'advanced technology products' (ATPs) exposes another major vulnerability. Both China and investor countries are dependent on each other's markets in the production of ATPs, and any confrontational behaviour in cyberspace will risk fragile economic growth. According to Theodore Moran, as of 2010, foreign-invested enterprises accounted for more than 96 per cent of all Chinese ATP exports (Moran 2011). China's ATP imports from the United States and its allies are, moreover, more important to it than its ATP exports. China is slowly moving from low-skill-intensive to high-skill-intensive manufacturing products, which will only increase the mutual dependencies in this sector. In the United States, the creeping dependence of its systems on Chinese-produced components is high. That said, as Moran observes, Chinese-owned firms are losing in the export competition with foreign-invested multinationals in China.

Acute dependencies also exist in other sectors that are deemed to be part of the national critical infrastructure, such as telecommunications and electricity. In the latter, where the United States is investing in the Chinese nuclear energy sector to feed the latter's electricity grid, US companies provide critical know-how when it comes to information security aspects. In undersea cables, all owned or operated by foreign corporations, Shanghai is the node for more than half of China's international communications.

Yet the United States sees China as a cyber adversary. This case has been made in a number of places. One of the most prominent has been the 2011 report of the US National Counterintelligence Executive (ONCIX 2011). The report observed that China and Russia see themselves as 'strategic competitors with the United States', and 'are the most aggressive collectors of US economic information and technology', relying heavily on 'open source information, HUMINT [human intelligence], signals intelligence (SIGINT) and cyber operations – to include computer network intrusions and exploitation of insider access to corporate and proprietary networks'. Their purpose, the report suggests, is to advance their own 'national security and economic prosperity' by gaining a 'competitive edge over the United States and other rivals'. Since the communications backbone for this political economy (the internet) is now just two decades old, the international system is still adjusting its norms, institutions and policy settings, even as stakeholders continuously push the boundaries of the possible.

The October 2011 decision by the US Commerce Department to rebuff the bid by Huawei to build a wireless network for first responders in the United States offers one example of how this adversarial positioning affects the economic relations and technology transfer debate. At the time, Huawei was one of the world's leading telecoms providers, working in more than 140 countries. It was selling critical equipment to America's closest allies in Europe and Asia, but many in the United States wanted to block its expansion there on national security grounds. The warnings were raised on several occasions, including in a letter to the US president, Barack Obama, from eight US senators, citing Huawei's past trade with Saddam Hussein's Iraq, its current trade with Iran, and the risk that the Chinese government might plant secret code in some of the equipment that would undermine US national security. According to the letter: 'British, French, Australian, and Indian intelligence agencies have either investigated Huawei or expressed concern that its products could facilitate remote hacking and thereby compromise the integrity of the telecommunications networks in their countries.' This was of course technically possible. There have been precedents where it has been done with equipment from other providers.

Yet in spite of the notoriety accorded Huawei by US critics, the suspicions cannot overshadow the progressive increase in investments of both Chinese and US investors in each other's telecommunication markets. Also, the unprecedented US current account deficit, and US consumption behaviour financed abroad (to a large degree by China), have substantially limited the United States' policy options in that regard. The United States simply cannot threaten to cut off China's access to the US domestic market. While Huawei announced in 2013 its intention of pulling back in its bids for big contracts in the US market, this will only be a temporary position.

At the diplomatic level, pressure from the United States on China over its cyber espionage policies had been steadily growing since 2011, and this has deepened the adversarial sense in Beijing. The US pressure came to a head in a series of chilly blasts from Washington over several months in 2013. On 12 February, President Obama, without naming China, alluded to it as an enemy of the United States for seeking to occupy its critical infrastructure through cyber operations. The remarks came two days after leaks from a US intelligence estimate named China – again – as the most serious menace in the cyber domain. On 11 March, national security adviser Thomas Donilon issued three demands on China, which responded the next day saying it was prepared to talk. The following day, the director of national intelligence identified cyber threats to the United States as the number one threat, and talked of a 'soft war' against the United States in this domain. On 14 March, Obama raised the issue with President Xi Jinping in their first telephone call as heads of state. Then, on 18 March, China's premier surprisingly called on both China and the United States to stop making 'groundless accusations' about cyber attacks against each other. On 19 March, the US Treasury secretary, Jack Lew, discussed the issue when he met Xi in Beijing. One week later, President Obama signed a bill to exclude the purchase of IT products by US government agencies if any part of them is made by a Chinese corporation. The United States had never mounted such a robust diplomatic campaign against China in this field, nor had it ever appeared to stake so much of the entire US–China relationship on cyber issues. A disinterested bystander could have been forgiven for believing that China's cyber power and actions had become a serious threat to US national security and that a political crisis between the two countries was inevitable unless China changed course. By April 2013, the two countries had agreed to set up a working group on cyber issues in the framework of the bilateral Strategic and Economic Dialogue, led at Cabinet level (secretaries of State and Treasury on the US side).

China and the United States have already started cooperating in some sensitive military fields. For example, in 2008 the two countries set up a hotline to prevent misunderstandings becoming crises. This was the joint response to the deterioration of relations after various intelligence-related incidents, such the collision of a US spy plane with a Chinese fighter jet in 2001. This was the first time that China had agreed to such a link with another country. In June 2013, to handle such matters in cyberspace at the diplomatic level, China set up an office for cyber security affairs in its foreign ministry.

Do China's leaders actually believe that the country's level of dependence on the security of the internet and other international digital communications platforms is so high that it is forced to pursue cooperative behaviour with the United States rather than put at risk the fabric of its international economic ties? Or do they believe that China's economy is immune from serious damage that might be suffered by the United States if the latter were subject to a debilitating cyber attack, for which many Americans believe China is preparing? The latter statement is probably farther from current reality than the former. The leaders do most probably feel obliged to cooperate in cyberspace rather than risk the fabric of China's economic ties (Austin and Gady 2012). China's economy is almost certainly not immune from serious damage that could be brought on by a US cyber attack. The same is true for the United States, even if the extent of US dependence is higher and its degree of immunity lower than those of China.

We can be more certain about the shared interests when we look at the potential impact of cyber crime. This is an increasingly dangerous threat to the macro-economy of major states. As the US director of national intelligence, retired Lieutenant General James Clapper, observed in February 2011 in testimony to Congress, the United States is facing 'new security challenges across a swath of our economy' because new technologies, intended to underpin prosperity, 'are enabling those who would steal, corrupt, harm, or destroy public and private assets vital to our national interest'. This is linked to international organized crime, which, he said, was penetrating governments, degrading the rule of law and enhancing the ability of states to manipulate key commodities markets, such as oil.

At the enterprise level, the risk has gone from merely losing money through cyber theft to a threat to the long-term survival of companies. On the one hand, law enforcement mechanisms both domestically and internationally are seen to be on the losing side. Too many cyber criminals appear for now to be outside the reach of law enforcement. On the other hand, global businesses now face attacks on such a scale and of such a frequency that Board leaders are being forced to re-evaluate enterprise security and come to terms with new risk management strategies. For major businesses, the cyber risks, vulnerabilities and threats are now as multinational as their corporate footprint, with the added character of being quite complex and difficult to anticipate. This is as true for Chinese enterprises operating globally, such as Huawei, as it is for similar US corporations.

The United States has taken a negative view of the thrust of China's cyber diplomacy. In its annual report in 2013 to Congress on China's military power, the DoD noted that 'Beijing's agenda is frequently in line with Russia's efforts to promote more international control over cyber activities'. Its assessment was that the Information Security Code of Conduct put forward by China and Russia 'would have governments exercise sovereign authority over the flow of information and control of content in cyberspace'. The report went on to say that 'both governments also continue to play a disruptive role in multilateral efforts to establish transparency and confidence-building measures' and that this was happening across the board, including in the Organization for

Security and Co-operation in Europe (OSCE), the Regional Forum of the Association of Southeast Asian Nations (ASEAN) and the UN group of governmental experts (GGE) on information security.

If both countries want stability and an end to current destabilizing cyber practices, the overarching policy question then becomes one of comparing insecurities and vulnerabilities, and later eventually addressing them. The two countries appear to need a strategy for managing a very big asymmetry of military power in cyberspace. There is little hint of that consideration in the bilateral diplomacy so far. A heavier emphasis on how concepts of common security can be applied in the bilateral cyber relationship to help end the divide between China and the United States may be needed. China's leaders (like their US counterparts) have yet to make a strong commitment in practice to this.

INTERDEPENDENT INFORMATIZED SECURITY

One of the more transformative aspects of the advent of the information society has been the entanglement of the military, economic and personal spheres in a seemingly borderless (non-national) cyberspace. This section looks first at how China's leaders have adapted their diplomatic posture to manage what they see as unique features of the information age, especially higher levels of interdependence. It then looks at their values on the question of cooperative action against common threats advanced information technologies.

While pursuing a self-reliant military posture for IW, China's government has articulated a complementary vision of national security in the information age that promotes cooperation across the geopolitical divides. On the one hand, this has been rooted in China's economic and technological needs for international technology, investment and trade. On the other hand, it has been equally rooted in recognition that the information age brings security problems that demand international cooperation.

In the years between 1995 and 1999, China had to begin to develop diplomatic strategies in connection with the emergent 'information society' concept, especially a G7 initiative in 1995 that led to an international conference in South Africa in 1996 on 'Information Society and Development', with the participation of more than forty countries and international organizations. In December 1998, China supported a UN General Assembly (UNGA) Resolution, the first on this subject, on the security aspects of information and communications technology (UN Docs A/RES/53/70, 4 December 1998). The resolution cited three drivers: optimization of exploitation of the technologies for development through broad international cooperation; the need to prevent the technologies being used for purposes inconsistent with international stability and the security of states; and the need to prevent the misuse of information resources or technologies for criminal or terrorist purposes. At the same UNGA session, China supported a resolution on Information in the Service of Humanity (A/Res/53/59, 3 December 1998) that called for freedom of the press, a diverse media and rapid transfer to developing countries of information technologies. In December 1999, China supported another resolution on the security aspects of information and communications technology (reiterating the 1998 text). In the intervening year, China did not join ten other states that submitted a report pursuant to the call in the 1998 resolution.

In making their commitment to an information society in 2000, the leaders were cognizant of key diplomatic implications. That year, Jiang Zemin appealed in very brief references, in both domestic and international settings, for a global internet convention in order to strengthen information security management jointly, 'to give full play to the positive role of the Internet' (Jiang 2010). His interventions coincided with the emergence in the G8 framework of the Okinawa Declaration on a Global Information Society in 2000, which sought to promote a globally inclusive approach, but which remained largely a G8 exercise, including through its Digital Opportunity Task Force. China did not have a fully articulated diplomatic strategy for international security aspects of the information society beyond those that affected economic settings, science and technology or domestic security. Nevertheless, it was actively trying to position itself in the diplomatic space, especially with reference to internet governance and the Internet Corporation for Assigned Names and Numbers (ICANN). Table 5.1 lists a few examples from 2000.

China could not avoid deepening diplomatic engagement in cooperative measures in cyberspace. In 2001, it joined APEC leaders in a statement that called for strengthening cooperation at all levels in counter-terrorism, including the protection of critical infrastructure, such as telecommunications. In 2002, APEC telecommunications ministers released the Shanghai Declaration, its associated Statement on the Security of Information and Communications Infrastructures, and a Programme of Action. The last document provided an impetus for convening expert groups on security-related issues. These early moves were largely declaratory but nonetheless provided a strong

Table 5.1: Selected additional international policy milestones, 2000

Regional Office for City Informatization in the Asia Pacific set up in Shanghai

CAS researcher elected unanimously as council chairman of Asia Pacific Top Level Domain Association

Chinese candidate for ICANN council membership fails to secure a seat

China supports new UNGA resolution on countering crime that relies on information technologies

China supports separate existing UNGA resolutions on information in the service of humanity and developments in the field of information and telecommunications foundation for a leading role later by China's diplomats in regional organizations.

At the first meeting of the Intergovernmental Preparatory Committee of the WSIS in 2002, China staked out its ground more firmly and more comprehensively. The speech by the Chinese delegate, Sha Zhukang, mentioned in chapter 1, articulated the need for innovations in diplomacy in order to respond to the information society, in particular: 'establishing international organisations and mechanisms that ensure the security and reliability of communication networks by fighting against viruses and cyber crimes' (Sha 2002). He offered an assessment of the current global situation with respect to the information society and then laid out a six-point position.

This was his assessment of the situation. Alongside unprecedented technological conditions for global economic and social development, informatization development around the world was 'seriously unbalanced'. The digital divide was 'widening instead of narrowing, putting the developing countries in a more disadvantageous position'. He warned that this would 'inevitably further aggravate the social and economic disparity' and that the digital divide had to become a major focal point of international action.

His six action points, some mentioned briefly in chapter 1, were:

- countries have different social and cultural traditions and different levels of economic development and informatization, so their plans and measures for informatization 'may well differ'
- considerable support will be needed by developing countries to 'accelerate their information infrastructure build-out'
- security is a multi-level problem, from promoting consumer confidence to countering terrorism, and involving technologies as well as laws and regulations that would require international cooperation
- new training and human resources would be needed

- developed countries should 'truly shoulder their responsibilities' by providing financial support, technology transfer and human resources training to developing countries
- while the private sector and civil society would need to be closely involved in creating the information society, when it came to the international policy stage, 'governments obviously should play the leading role'.

Subsequently, China started to firm up its commitment to the goals of common security in an interdependent cyberspace. This can be seen in its support for the December 2002 UNGA Resolution (A/Res/57/239) on 'Creation of a Global Culture of Cybersecurity' and for the 2003 Geneva Declaration of Principles on the WSIS. The earlier UN resolutions, beginning in 1998, had the effect of saying that information technologies were of concern to international and national security, whereas the annual resolutions of 2002 and 2003 saw China signing up to gradually more explicit statements of what that meant and what should be done about it with other states.

In its first response to the UN secretary-general's call in 1998 for states to register their views on international measures for information security, China made a fairly strong if short intervention in 2004. It said that 'information security has become a grave challenge in the field of international security'. It had taken six years to respond to the call, but China further declared its support for international efforts to promote the 'information security of all countries'. It also supported the establishment of a group of governmental experts to discuss how common understandings on the issues might be advanced at the international level. The statement called for special attention to 'information criminality and terrorism'. It reiterated the view that the 'imbalanced development of countries in the field of telecommunications' mandated a need for the international community to deepen cooperation in the research and application of information technology (UN Docs A/59/116, 23 June 2004).

In a statement to the UN in 2006, China was much firmer on the need for states to respect the differences in political systems, asserting that the principle of the free flow of information 'should be guaranteed under the premises that national sovereignty and security must be safeguarded and that the historical, cultural and political differences among countries be respected'. It asserted its doctrine that there is a legally bounded, national cyberspace, and therefore a Chinese internet: 'each country has the right to manage its own cyberspace in accordance with its domestic legislation'. It repeated the call for developed countries to help the poorer ones, but invoked a new international right: the 'freedom of information technology'. It positively appraised the work of the first GGE for its 'profound exchange of ideas' and 'numerous valuable proposals', even though it had failed to produce a consensus report. China indicated its support for reconvening a similar group in 2009 (UN Docs A/61/161, 18 July 2006).

Henceforth China would be more active. It sought a leading role in international governance of telecommunications and the internet when its candidate, Zhao Houlin, was elected deputy secretary-general of the ITU in 2006, the first official from China to hold such a senior post in the organization. According to information from the Ministry of Foreign Affairs, it appears that China had stepped up its engagement in the ITU only in 2002 (having not paid it much attention since it regained the China seat thirty years earlier). It appears to have done this in response to a wide range of international and domestic developments affecting cyberspace.

In July 2006, the ASEAN Regional Forum (ARF), which included China, issued a statement that its members should implement cyber crime and cyber security laws 'in accordance with their national conditions and by referring to relevant international instruments'. The ARF has also called on its members to collaborate in addressing criminal misuse of cyberspace, including by terrorists. Around this time, China, Japan and South Korea separately agreed a work plan that 'includes projects on network and information security policies and mechanisms, joint response to cyber attacks (including hacking and viruses), information exchange on online privacy protection information, and creation of a Working Group to promote this cooperation'. Also in 2006, the APEC telecommunications ministers agreed on a new structure aimed at more effective responses to the full suite of global challenges by establishing three steering groups: (economic) liberalization, ICT development, and security and prosperity.

China took a more dramatic step in 2006 when it joined a declaration by the Shanghai Cooperation Organization (SCO) on information security. Alongside China, Russia and four states of Central Asia with authoritarian governments make up the SCO, so this declaration allowed China to mobilize international support around its positions on most issues, especially the balance to be struck between state sovereignty and international openness.

In 2009, China and ASEAN signed a framework agreement on network and information security emergency response, and the SCO formally agreed a treaty on the subject. This was the first international treaty on information security that went beyond cyber crime and specifically addressed the range of security issues that had been canvassed in UN resolutions. The APEC Working Group on Telecommunications agreed an action plan for 2010–15 that included 'fostering a safe and trusted ICT environment', the security of networked systems, sharing best practice approaches, joint technical cooperation, and cyber security awareness initiatives. The plan committed members to work with industry. In its 2010 white paper on the internet, China reaffirmed its earlier international commitments to collaborate internationally for cyber security.

In January 2011, the United States and China committed for the first time at head-of-state level to work together on a bilateral basis to address issues of cyber security. Although this was merely a passing mention among some twenty issues listed in one long sentence of a document several pages in length, it was an important first mention, coming thirteen years after a similar first mention in a presidential communiqué between the US and Russian presidents (Gady and Austin 2010). In a 2011 speech to the UN, China's ambassador acknowledged the seriousness of the impact of the information age on security: 'information and cyberspace security represents a major non-traditional security challenge confronting the international community. Effective response to this challenge has become an important element of international security' (Wang Qun 2011). The ambassador went on to say that states should view this issue from the new perspective of 'a community of common destiny' and 'work together towards a peaceful, secure and equitable information and cyber space'. This approach contrasts quite strongly with that of mainstream military strategists in China. It is equivalent to the shift by the Soviet Union under Gorbachev to the idea of common security, a shift that was essential for ending the Cold War. Wang advocated five principles that together represent a comprehensive statement of the country's view on the diplomatic aspects of international security in the information age. The US secretary of state Hillary Clinton had made a similarly ground-breaking exposition of her country's view in January 2010. Ambassador Wang was making his response with the five principles, each of which covered several items:

- *peace*: war avoidance, preventive diplomacy, and promotion of the use of information technology in maintaining security; commitment to non-use of information and cyber technology for hostile actions; non-proliferation of information weapons; retention of the right of self-defence against 'threats, disturbance, attack and sabotage'; prevention of a cyber arms race; and commitment to peaceful settlement of disputes

- *sovereignty*: states to remain the main actor in governance of information and cyberspace; sovereignty and territorial integrity to remain basic norms; countries to build a comprehensive and integrated national management system for all aspects of cyberspace; cyber technology not to be used as 'another tool to interfere in internal affairs of other countries'
- *balance between freedom and security*: the rule of law to be upheld to keep order in information and cyberspace; practising power politics in cyberspace in the name of cyber freedom untenable
- *cooperation*: interdependence of cyber networks, meaning that 'no country is able to manage only its own information and cyber business' or 'ensure its information and cyber security by itself'; all countries to work together
- *equitable development*: developed countries' obligation 'to help developing countries enhance capacity in information and cyber technology and narrow the digital divide.'

To promote this policy agenda on the international stage, China and several other countries (Russia, Tajikistan and Uzbekistan) submitted to the UNGA in 2011 a proposal for an International Code of Conduct for Information Security. Russia, not China, was the driving force in this initiative, but it nevertheless represented a new level of international mobilization by China. These proposals go close, in part, to matching the list of ideal values in the field of national security: strategic stability, bridging the two-camps divide, and committing to joint solutions to global problems (e.g. climate change) relying on informatized assets. They received further expression in a speech on 5 July 2012 by the vice-minister of foreign affairs, Cui Tankai, to the Asia Society in Hong Kong: 'we believe countries should build mutual trust and seek common security . . . Security at the expense of others will only make us less secure.'

China had by now entered full fighting mode with the United States and its allies on issues of global internet governance. This was seen in an intensification of its campaign in the UN but also in a strong move to have responsibility for the internet at the intergovernmental level taken by the ITU, and not by non-governmental organizations such as the Internet Engineering Task Force, ICANN and the Internet Society. The debate reached a climax of sorts in December 2012 at the World Conference on International Telecommunications when a group of countries, including China, tried to extend the coverage of International Telecommunications Regulations (ITRs) to include the internet. This was in strong opposition to the United States and like-minded countries, which were opposed to what they saw as mission creep by the ITU and an attempt by China and its allies to assert anti-libertarian political control over the future development of the internet. While the issue appeared to have been settled in pre-conference negotiations, the meeting came to a stormy end with a walkout by the US delegation and some allied delegations in protest at the late tabling of a draft resolution that would allow intergovernmental consultations on certain aspects of internet governance. This did not stop eighty-nine countries from signing the resolution and amending the ITRs.

The sharp edges of the debate were ameliorated marginally by China's hosting in April 2013 of the 46th meeting of ICANN in Beijing, at which the ICANN chairman, Stephen Crocker, announced the opening of its first Global Engagement Office (one of several planned around the world) in Beijing. But the dispute on the fundamentals of global internet governance between the two camps is still in play.

In this environment, the goal of cooperation between China on the one hand and the United States and its allies on the other may seem remote. But the confrontation in the political domain is in strong contrast with the situation in other areas of policy, especially economic and social. The gathering momentum in this area has been captured in a series of UNGA agreements and resolutions, especially the December 2011 Resolution adopted by the General Assembly on the report of the Second Committee (UN Docs A/66/437) on Information and Communications Technologies for Development, and an associated General Assembly resolution (UN Docs A/Res/66/184). In other areas, some headway has been made. For example, by the end of 2013, the annual Sino–US Internet Forum has been convened seven times. The US–China Joint Law Enforcement Liaison Group, though set up in 1998, had been progressively more active and effective after 2005, including in fighting cyber crime. In August 2011, it succeeded in a joint operation against a global child pornography network, shutting down eighteen websites after years of unsuccessful bilateral talks. Its meeting in late 2013 involved some eighty participants meeting over two days. In one Chinese view, there are several areas for relatively easy progress in multilateral diplomacy: emergency response to cyber security, supply chain security, submarine cable protection and action against groups like WikiLeaks, Anonymous, LulzSec and AntiSec (Yi Wenli 2012).

At the practical level, there is substantial cooperation between organizations and individuals in China and other countries in ventures for economic and social development that can be IT-enabled, and this holds out the prospect of considerable positive impact for the affected communities. Key actors include the Gates Foundation, Rockefeller Foundation, Cisco and Microsoft. The investments may be small in dollar terms compared with the overall size of the Chinese economy, but they are symbolically important as examples of cooperative problem solving. One of the most notable is the smart cities project developed by Cisco for global application and executed in China since 2009, under an agreement with the municipality of Chongqing (a city with the status of province). Cisco is supporting the city's goal of providing a comprehensive set of e-government services (in education, health care and public safety) and implementing a number of green development strategies. In terms of international activities, the Chinese government and some corporations have started to take a role in capacity building for informatization in a number of policy areas, not least internal security and basic information security, and especially in poorer countries either on its periphery (such as Kyrgyzstan) or further afield in Africa.

On the international stage, the leaders of China have placed informatization at the very top of their operational principles in national security policy. They are, however, still at the early stages of consistently framing, and promoting in national security debates on the domestic stage, the 'cooperative' or 'common security' view of the ethical implications of informatization. As mentioned earlier, it was only in June 2013 that the Foreign Ministry set up an office to deal with the diplomacy of cyber security. At a more ideal level, the concept for the future has been laid out by a military researcher as follows: 'war ethics will play a more important role in the long run . . . being a responsible big power, China should shoulder the big flag of international morality and justice, act actively as the cooperator and main participant of the existing ethics order, and turn progressively into constitutor and dominator of rules' (Li 2012). Yet it is far from clear that Chinese strategic policy and the operations of its armed forces, both set largely by the CMC, are as in tune with such an internationalist vision.

CONCLUSION

Since the turn of the century, China has moved only slowly, though in a reasonably deliberate manner, to adjust its legacy values in international security affairs to match the ideal policy values of the information age more closely.

Strategic stability: The leaders retained a strong commitment in principle to a stable world order but were becoming more confident that the country's rising military and economic power gave them a much stronger hand to play. They wanted a continuation of peace for development, but they really wanted an adjustment of the balance of power more in their favour. They had become committed to positioning the country for long-term cyber military power, and China had become an aggressive actor in cyber espionage (like other major powers). There was nonetheless a conflict in these values and it continued to play itself out in China's acceptance that it somehow had to reassure major powers that its emerging cyber power was not aggressively motivated.

Bridging military divides: By early 2014, China had a deepening commitment to peaceful integration with Taiwan because this strategy was working. In just one decade after 2002, China had replaced the United States as Taiwan's main economic partner. Here, one ethical setting of China's leaders has been profoundly important: Chinese should not fight Chinese. This is highly consistent with the corresponding ideal value needed for an information society. And the payoffs for China have been spectacular. While this could not paper over residual sharp differences of values with Taiwanese leaders, the bridging appeared to be at least entering its final stages. In principle China remained opposed to military alliances and confrontation with major powers, but its adversarial view of the United States had deepened considerably.

Interdependent informatized security: China was committed in principle and practice to cooperative norms in economic and technological aspects of the global information economy. It had strengthened its commitment to joint problem solving in non-military domains, but it had not been able to bridge its formidable differences with the United States and like-minded countries over internet governance.

So, overall, how do China's leaders evaluate their evolving security situation in the global infosphere? In terms of informatization of its armed forces, the leaders acknowledge that they have a long way to go, though the basic settings are gradually being put in place. Their timetable of 2050 for full informatization should be attainable. China may have had considerable successes in cyber espionage, but so too have its potential adversaries. China's moves in late 2013 to tighten network and data security in reaction to the Snowden revelations of NSA successes against China are evidence enough of that. Moreover, its inability to make an appreciable dint in the 'information superiority' of the US global alliance will remain a source of considerable anxiety for its leaders. Few outside China have been prepared to credit its leaders with a reasonable concern about the threatening impacts on its military and domestic security of the rapid development of advanced cyber military capabilities by the United States and its allies. Few have been prepared to discuss the likely impacts on China's sense of insecurity of US cyber capability to disrupt or even disable Chinese nuclear and conventional force command and control. In this environment, China has wanted to improve its military capability for a number of contingencies progressively and as part of its overall national power ambition.

As much as China's race for capability in this domain may be understandable, it has also been destabilizing its relationships. So, at another level, the need for common diplomatic understandings of how to manage the emerging realities of military cyberspace has become an important priority for the leaders. Beginning in 2000, China has shown its willingness to play a cooperative role in international governance of cyberspace, including on some security issues. Yet, in the same way that the entire international community has come late to finding the right balance between a classic adversarial construction of national security in cyberspace and a more internationalist, interdependent conception, China too is a relatively new entrant to that field. The challenge for its leaders will be to stake out the internationalist vision more effectively over the heads of its military and security chiefs, who remain concerned about US cyber dominance.

Thus, for all of the period from 2000, China's leaders have never once in practice seen themselves as having the luxury of strategic stability in cyberspace, as much as they may have valued it in principle. They felt themselves obliged to participate in an emerging cyber arms race in which they were starting from a long way behind. This inferior starting position was in itself a destabilizing condition. Almost everything China's leaders said and did about international governance and military development in cyberspace seemed, rightly or wrongly, to have a destabilizing effect because of the overarching environment of militarization of cyberspace. When it comes to international negotiations over internet governance, China's leaders are in a combative mood. This was illustrated dramatically in late February 2014 when, as mentioned earlier, it emerged that for the first time the general secretary of the CCP, in the person of Xi Jinping, would head the leadership group on informatization (formerly called the SILG) in order especially to protect national security better.

6   The Road Ahead ——————

Since deciding in 2000 that China must become an advanced information society, the country's leaders have at different times gone on record supporting in some measure each one of the nine policy values held up in this book to be essential for realizing such an ambition. These are listed in table 1.2 and provided the framework for this analysis. Since 2000, the leaders have been consistently self-critical in broad terms of their own policy dispositions that have undercut their ambition. They have referred to the need to be more faithful to the overarching goal either of achieving an information society or simply of comprehensive informatization. Thus, the idea that what is good for the information society is good for China has some resonance with its leaders. As Xi Jinping said on 27 February 2014, on taking over the lead in all cyber policy: 'No informatization means no modernization.' He also laid out a long list of shortcomings in cyber policy, all of which have been highlighted in this analysis. He said China had to address these so that it could become a 'cyber power' (网络大国 wǎngluò dàguó). His timeframe was the two-step approach mentioned earlier for PLA informatization (2020/2050), but he linked it to the 'two hundreds' theme in his idea of the China dream: moderate informatization by the hundredth anniversary of the CCP in 2021 and full informatization by the hundredth anniversary of the founding of the PRC in 2049.

In the area of free exchange of information and protecting that exchange, China's leaders have followed a dual policy. On the one hand, there has been amazing and inspiring progress in the sheer volume and types of information that became newly available to Chinese for the first time as their information revolution took hold. In this environment, the leaders come to accept, in principle at least, ideas of e-democracy and open government, holding out the promise both of participatory or consultative democracy and of access to information on how the country is governed.

On the other hand, these processes of e-democracy and transparency peaked early and appear to be stalled. China remains a nontransparent country. The leaders have maintained a policy of dictator's control within an atypical environment of highly liberalized mass communication. So it has looked deceptively different from previous dictatorships, but there should be no confusion: China remains an i-dictatorship. The leaders became less focused on opposing a broad sweep of ideas and critical commentary, and this has been a small miracle in itself. Yet the new technologies allowed them to detect and silence at an earlier stage those people who might organize a political or social movement around opposing ideas. The leaders' use of advanced technologies and armies of censors to suppress errant statements, and their purveyors, appears to be 100 per cent inconsistent with the information society ambition. The information ecosystem in China is anything but trusting and secure. The leaders have not demonstrated a strong commitment to the idea that information that matters to its citizens should be freely accessible and widely exchanged, or the idea that such exchange should enjoy strong protection in the legal system.

In pursuing an innovative information economy, the leaders have demonstrated similar dualism. They have committed to the idea of a transformative and innovative information economy. China's corporations, such as Huawei and ZTE, have gone global. Yet the leaders have not liberalized and empowered several key drivers of social and scientific innovation, especially universities. They have confused manufacturing prowess with technological innovation; they have prioritized innovation in machine building (supercomputers) at the expense of social innovation; and they have maintained a nationally bounded concept of innovation, which favours the domestic over the foreign. They have removed the stultifying hand of Party control from private business but not from key centres of knowledge and social innovation.

In managing China's national security in the global information ecosystem, there has been one remarkable success story. This is the way in which the deepening relationship with Taiwan over twenty years, especially in the ICT sector, has bridged the very strong two-camps divide that defined their relationship after 1949. But when it comes to wider international settings, leadership values towards cyberspace have only exacerbated the two-camps divide with the United States. While the leaders have articulated a framing of national security that situates the country in a secure and cooperative international system, they have not followed through on that in their policy decisions. One reason for this failure is that they feel obliged to participate in a cyber arms race that they feel they did not start. Yet it would appear that their preferred framing for now (their default value) is an adversarial one. While the US push for the technological frontier of cyber military power is aggravating the negative tendency, China's leaders have also allowed their sense of vulnerability to aggravate tensions. This negative trend has emerged in spite of countervailing forces, particularly an increasingly open international economy and WTO membership, which have been fuelling the spectacularly cooperative economic relations.

These conclusions leave room for us to return to the departure point of the book – the idea of a transformational information society in China – with a more critical eye. Should we see it as an all-embracing and dominating system (the radical, transformationalist view), or as just one part of a larger society in which a range of other issues, such as political power, land ownership, urbanization or industrial hollowing-out, might seem to be of higher priority? The latter policy approach (informatization as just one of several strands of policy) may be more appealing because it is more familiar. Most Chinese leaders certainly identify instinctively with it. But this is their dilemma. They say they want an advanced information society that is transformational (the radical view) but, as this analysis has shown, they situate that ambition in a mixed bag of competing ambitions, where the priority attached to individual elements changes all too often. Their policy values are very conflicted.

Whether China eventually becomes an advanced information society or not will ultimately be determined by a range of political, economic, social and legal factors, all with domestic as well as international dimensions. It will not be decided exclusively by leaders of the Communist Party. But at this stage of history, the CCP leaders are still playing a very influential role that gives a green light for progress down certain pathways, while giving a red or amber light for others. This plays directly into the attitudes of innovators inside and outside China. Why labour in China when there are other, more welcoming places to work, where the rewards are better and there are reasonable standards of legal protection?

The Chinese political system (the Party-state apparatus) has some features that advantage pursuit by the leaders of the information society ambition. This system has proven to be adaptive and there has been a steady stream of remarkable institutional innovations. The most remarkable included the dismantling of the agricultural communes, the re-establishment of private property, the opening of the Communist Party to business leaders, and the decision to join the WTO on terms negotiated with the United States. China's embrace of globalization has been surprising and against the grain of its modern history. The government did lift the heavy hand of the state off individual choice by eliminating many controls, such as the right of decision over where one worked or studied, and for people to choose their own housing. The leaders have presided over a massive liberalization and pluralization of the society, exemplified first by allowing and then fostering the growth of civil society organizations and criticism of the government through 'democratic supervision'. The liberalization has occurred in large part because of the leaders' willingness to allow privately owned media operations (including foreign media) and a flourishing internet culture (albeit censored). The economy has developed in ways that have created much opportunity for individual fulfilment for those who could benefit.

Yet the political system that is for now commanding the pace of development of the information society in China is not by nature an innovative one, nor is it transparent and informational. It does not allow freedom of association, an independent legal system, organized political opposition to the one-Party state, or even sustained organized opposition to government policy by civil society groups on non-political issues.

We can see some agreement at the highest levels in China about the character of the domestic challenges involved in resetting policy to achieve the information society ambitions. The former prime minister Wen Jiabao told a press conference on the sidelines of the NPC in March 2012 that 'without a successful political reform, it's impossible for China to fully institute economic reform and the gains we have made in these areas may be lost'. While Wen did not say it, this applies as much to the information society ambition as to others. In his formal work report to the NPC, Wen replayed many of the important themes outlined above. The same sort of sentiments were expressed in the CCP's sixty-point reform agenda of November 2013.

As Ken Lieberthal observed in a 2004 publication and as recently as a TV interview aired in China on 10 December 2012, the country has been good at making organizational change but probably needs to do better at building social institutions (Lieberthal 2004). By that he meant institutions that endure beyond political cycles because they have an independent status and a stature that ensures their ability to survive and strengthens their influence. The best example of this in

China may be the CAS. For the information society ambition, there are several other sets of institutions that count as well: the legal system and the education system being two of the most important.

Does China have to wait for new leaders to quicken the pace of transition to an information society? Does it have to wait for a collapse of the Communist Party for the information society ambition to be advanced more decisively? The answer to that is: not necessarily. The Party state can oversee the transition to an advanced information society and probably retain its power if it begins to adhere more closely to the nine ideal policy values. Singapore, which has been ruled by one political party continuously since its independence in 1965, today ranks very high in most international comparisons of a country's information readiness. Could a one-party system like that in Singapore be as conducive (perhaps more so) to the achievement of the goal of an advanced information society as a multi-party system? The answer may be yes. But it would have to be a one-party state that gives a very high priority to the nine ideal values, as Singapore does.

If the obstacles to the information society ambition in China are political values, then the only way for the CCP to achieve its objective is to change its political values, and adopt ones that are consistent with the ambition. If this CCP has been able to admit capitalists, restore private property and even partially privatize SOEs, then surely it has the wit and the capacity to move more aggressively to build the institutions that promote an advanced and open information society. But it has to have the right ethical setting. It has come to where it is today largely on pragmatism, but now it needs firmer political values (the ethics) that match the information society ambition.

There is a visible tension within the leadership about values. China is as close to a tipping point in this area of policy as it could be. In 2013, the leaders realized this and clamped down very firmly on FOI, on journalists and on rules for commentary on the internet.

My best judgement is that by 2025 China's leaders will have opted in favour of better choices. By then, we will probably not be debating whether China is likely to overtake the technological lead of the United States. That will not be anyone's highest priority because it is a pipe dream. Knowledge has no flag. The content of GDP is not purely national any more, if it ever was. By 2025, we will be more interested in whether the two countries are working together in a global info-sphere as effectively as they can to marshal shared information assets in the fight against global and national problems, including such basic challenges as fresh water availability and climate stability. China looks set to become an advanced information society on a par with other developed countries within several decades. However, current indications are that to arrive at that point, there will probably need to be some sort of crisis to push China's relatively new leadership out of the ethical dead end into which it has been marched. China needs new thinking from its leaders, a clear shift to ideas of common security, if it is to enjoy the sustainable prosperity that the capabilities of an advanced information society can offer. Only a stronger embrace of the spirit of the information age – full transparency in governance at home and deeper integration with a free and open international knowledge society – will deliver on China's ambitions.

References

In researching this book, around 1,000 sources were consulted. These included government documents, policy reports, academic studies, books and website articles. At the request of the publisher, to make the list manageable for this short book, three types of references are omitted: those that are cited only because they have documented factual events, including speeches or statements of government policy, that can be easily verified; references to website statements about the missions of various organizations; and UN documents. Where appropriate, these are clearly referenced through the text by date and source but without weblinks.

All website references in this list were reconfirmed on 30 December 2013.

AI (Amnesty International) (2006) Undermining freedom of expression in China: The role of Yahoo!, Microsoft and Google. http://www.amnesty.org/en/library/asset/POL30/026/2006/en/18c6f357-d41b-11dd-8743-d305bea2b2c7/pol300262006en.html.

Anon. (1972) *Computing in China: A Travel Report* [by six American computer scientists invited by the People's Republic of China]. http://digitalcollections.library.cmu.edu/awweb/awarchive?type=file&item=74954.

Austin, Greg (2001) China's power: Searching for stable domestic foundations. In Zhang, Y. and Austin, G. (eds.), *Chinese Foreign Policy: Motivations, Power and Responsibility*. Asia Pacific Press, Canberra, 69–104.

Austin, Greg and Gady, Franz (2012) *Cyber Detente between the United States and China*. EastWest Institute, New York/Brussels/Moscow.

Ball, Desmond (2011) China's cyber warfare capabilities. *Security Challenges*, 7(2), 81–103.

Bandurski, David (2013) Managing the hazards of online society. *China Media Project*, 13 May. http://cmp.hku.hk/2013/05/13/33042.

Bao Xiaohui, Xu Xiaofan, Li Cheming, Yuan Zhensheng, Lu Chaoyang and Pan Jianwei (2012) Quantum teleportation between remote atomic-ensemble quantum memories. Cornell University Library. Submitted 13 November. http://arxiv.org/abs/1211.2892.

Bell, Daniel (1976) *The Coming of Post-Industrial Society*. Harper Colophon Books, New York.

Bell, Mark R. and Boas, Taylor C. (2003) Falung Gong and the internet: evangelism, community and struggle for survival. *Nova Religio*, 6, 277–93.

Benney, Jonathon (2013) *Defending Rights in Contemporary China*. Routledge, London.

Bradsher, Keith (2013) Next made-in-China boom: College graduates. *New York Times*, 16 January. http://www.nytimes.com/2013/01/17/business/chinas-ambitious-goal-for-boom-in-college-graduates.html?pagewanted=all&_r=0.

Breschi, Stefani and Malerba, Franco (1997) Sectoral innovation systems. In Edquist, C. (ed.), *Systems of Innovation: Technologies, Institutions and Organizations*. Pinter/Cassell, London, 130–56.

Breznitz, Dan (2007) *Innovation and the State: Political Choices and Strategies for Growth in Israel, Taiwan and Ireland*. Yale University Press, New Haven CT.

Brock, Darryl E. (2009) Science innovation during the Cultural Revolution: Notes from the *Peking Review*. *Southeast Review of Asian Studies*, 31, 226–32.

BSA (Software Alliance) (2013) *2013 BSA Global Cloud Computing Scorecard: A Clear Path to Progress*. Software Alliance and Galexia Consulting. http://cloudscorecard.bsa.org/2013/index.html.

CAS (2009) *Technological Revolution and China's Future: Innovation 2050*. http://english.bic.cas.cn/NE/200906/t20090619_7263.html.

CASS (2007) *Surveying internet Usage and its Impact in Seven Chinese cities: China Internet Project Survey Report*. http://www.markle.org/news-events/media-releases/chinese-turn-internet-entertainment-and-connecting-others-number-broadban.

Castells, Manuel (2012) *Networks of Outrage and Hope: Social Movements in the Internet Age*. Polity, Cambridge.

Castells, Manuel (2005) The network society: From knowledge to policy. In Castells, M. and Cardoso, G. (eds.), *The Network Society: From Knowledge to Policy*. Johns Hopkins Center for Transatlantic Relations, Washington DC, 3–21.

CC&M (China Copyright and Media) (2013) Secret central committee document calls for loyalty, warns for Western influence. 14 May. http://

chinacopyrightandmedia.wordpress.com/2013/05/14/secret-central-committee-document-calls-for-loyalty-warns-for-western-influence.

CECC (Congressional-Executive Commission on China) (2010) Top Chinese security officials urge continued crackdown in 2010. 12 February. http://www.cecc.gov/pages/virtualAcad/index.phpd?showsingle=135611.

Central Committee (2013) CCP Central Committee resolution concerning some major issues in comprehensively deepening reform, passed at the 3rd Plenum of the 18th Central Committee of the Chinese Communist Party on 12 November. 15 November. http://chinacopyrightandmedia.wordpress.com/2013/11/15/ccp-central-committee-resolution-concerning-some-major-issues-in-comprehensively-deepening-reform.

Central Committee and State Council (2006) CPC Central Committee and State Council on issuing the 2006–2020 National Development Strategy [in Chinese]. http://www.china.com.cn/chinese/PI-c/1203246.htm.

Chao Xueqin, Gao Xiaoyu and Ma Dongyan (2012) Analysis of China's downgrade in informatization development indexes in an international comparative study. In *Analysis and Forecast on China's Informatization (2012): Blue Book of China's Informatization*. Social Sciences and Academic Press, Beijing [in Chinese], 324–42.

Chen, Huijie and Chu, Heting (1995) Chinese information market: Seamless networking in China – progress, problems and perspectives. *Bulletin of the American Society for Information Science*. http://www.asis.org/Bulletin/Jun-95/chen.html.

Cheng Li (2012) Introduction. In He Weifang, *In the Name of Justice: Striving for the Rule of Law in China*. Brookings Institution, Washington DC, xvii–xlix.

Cheng Li (2013) Rule of the princelings. *Brookings Research*, 10 February. http://www.brookings.edu/research/articles/2013/02/china-xi-jinping-li.

Chiu, Joanna (2013) Censored Sina Weibo posts translated into English by HKU project. *South China Morning Post*, 14 May. http://www.scmp.com/news/china/article/1237117/censored-sina-weibo-posts-translated-english-hku-project.

Cisco (2002) *Overview of the Public Security Sector.* http://www.wired.com/images_blogs/threatlevel/files/cisco_presentation.pdf.

Clarke, Richard A. and Knake, Robert K. (2010) *Cyber War: The Next Threat to National Security and What to Do About It.* HarperCollins, New York.

Cliff, Roger, Fei, John F., Hagen, Jeff, Hague, Elizabeth, Heginbotham, Eric and Stillion, John (2011) *Shaking the Heavens and Splitting the Earth: Chinese Air Force Employment Concepts in the 21st Century.* Rand, Santa Monica CA.

CNCERT (2013) *Annual Report 2012.* http://www.cert.org.cn/publish/english/ 115/2013/20130716100050563462704/20130716100050563462704_. html.

CNNIC (1986–2013) Internet timeline, available on several separate pages at http://www1.cnnic.cn/IDR/hlwfzdsj.

CNNIC (2013) *Statistical Report on Internet Development in China: 31st Semi-Annual Survey Report.* CNNIC, Beijing.

Dai Xiudan (2002) Towards a digital economy with Chinese characteristics? *New Media and Society,* 4, 141–61.

Deng Xiaoping (1980) Talk with some leading comrades of the Central Committee, 25 October. http://english.peopledaily.com.cn/dengxp/vol2/ text/b1420.html.

Deng Xiaoping (1979) Speech to the Central Committee, 30 March: Uphold the four cardinal principles. In translation, http://english.peopledaily.com.cn/ dengxp/vol2/text/b1290.html.

DHS (US Department of Homeland Security) (2012) Immigration statistics, tables 3, 7 and 8. http://www.dhs.gov/files/statistics/publications/LPR11. shtm.

DoD (US Department of Defense) (2013) *Military and Security Developments Involving the People's Republic of China 2013.* United States Dept of Defense, Washington DC.

DoD (US Department of Defense) (2012) *Military and Security Developments Involving the People's Republic of China 2012.* United States Dept of Defense, Washington DC.

DoD (US Department of Defense) (2011) *Military and Security Developments Involving the People's Republic of China, 2011.* United States Dept of Defense, Washington DC.

Dong Zhengwei (2013) Blog, 25 February. http://blog.sina.com.cn/s/ blog_57a1cb0701019wtf.html.

Duan Qing (2012) *China's IT Leadership: The Political Struggle behind China's Information Revolution.* Akademiker, Saarbrüchen.

Economist (2013) Security in Tibet: Grid locked. *Economist,* 22 June.

Esarey, Ashley and Xiao Qiang (2011) Digital communication and political change in China. *International Journal of Communication,* 5, 298–319.

Etzkowitz, Henry, Dzisah, James, Ranga, Marina and Zhou Chunyan (2007) University–industry–government interaction: The triple helix model for innovation. *Asia-Pacific Tech Monitor,* 24(1), 14–23.

Fang Lizhi (1989) The past and the future, trans. Perry Link. http://www. nybooks.com/articles/archives/2011/jun/23/past-and-future.

Farina, Claudio and Preissl, Brigitte (2000) *Research and Technology Organizations in National Systems of Innovation*. DIW Discussion Paper, 221. http://www.diw.de/documents/publikationen/73/38616/dp221.pdf.

Farrall, Kenneth Neil (2008) Global privacy in flux: Illuminating privacy across cultures in China and the U.S. *International Journal of Communication*, 2, 993–1030.

Finn, Michael B. (2010) *Stay Rates of Foreign Doctorate Recipients from U.S. Universities, 2007*. Oak Ridge Institute for Science and Education (ORISE). http://heglobal.international.gbtesting.net/media/7133/stay-rates-foreign-doctorate-recipients-2007.pdf.

Floridi, Luciano (2013) *The Ethics of Information*. Oxford University Press, Oxford.

Floridi, Luciano (2005) Information ethics, its nature and scope. In van den Hoven, J. and Weckert, J. (eds.), *Moral Philosophy and Information Technology*. Cambridge University Press, Cambridge, 40–65.

Floridi, Luciano and Sanders, J. W. (2002) Mapping the foundationalist debate in computer ethics. *Ethics and Information Technology*, 4(1), 1–9.

Frost, Mervyn (2009) *Global Ethics: Anarchy, Freedom and International Relations*. Routledge, New York.

Frost, Mervyn (1986) *Towards a Normative Theory of International Relations*. Cambridge University Press, Cambridge.

Fu Guangxin and Yan Shuzhen (2012) Information and regional economic growth: Taking the case of Shandong province. Paper presented at the 2012 Second International Conference on Business Computing and Global Informatization.

Fuller, Douglas B. (2008) The political economy of technological development in China's information technology sector. In Rowen, H. S., Hancock, M. and Miller, W. F. (eds.), *Greater China's Quest for Innovation*. Walter H. Shorenstein Asia-Pacific Research Center Books, Stanford CA, 85–108.

Gady, Franz Stefan and Austin, Greg (2010) *Russia, the United States, and Cyber Diplomacy: Opening the Doors*. EastWest Institute, New York/Brussels/Moscow.

Gereffi, Gary, Wadwha, Vivek and Rissing, Ben (2006) Framing the engineering outsourcing debate: Comparing the quantity and quality of engineering graduates in the United States, India and China. Paper prepared for SASE 2006 Conference, 'Constituting Globalisation: Actors, Arenas, and Outcomes', Trier, Germany, 30 June–2 July.

Hassan, Robert (2008) *The Information Society*. Polity, Cambridge.

Hayhoe, Ruth and Zha Qiang (2011) Peking University: Icon of cultural leadership. In Hayhoe, R., Li Jun, Lin Jing and Zha Qiang, *Portraits of 21st Century*

Chinese Universities: In the Move to Mass Higher Education. Springer, Dordrecht, 95–130.

Herold, David Kurt (2013) Captive artists: Chinese university students talk about the internet (1 May). http://ssrn.com/abstract=2259020.

Hjortdal, Magnus (2011) China's use of cyber warfare: Espionage meets strategic deterrence. *Journal of Strategic Security,* IV(2), 1–24.

Hu, Albert Guangzhou (2008) What do they patent in China, and why? In Rowen, H. S., Hancock, M. and Miller, W. F. (eds.), *Greater China's Quest for Innovation.* Walter H. Shorenstein Asia-Pacific Research Center Books, Stanford CA, 255–68.

Huang Lucheng, Wang Kangkang, Wu Feifei, Lou Yan, Miao Hong and Xu Yanmei (2012) SWOT analysis of information technology industry in Beijing, China using patent data. In Murgante, B. et al. (eds.), *ICCSA 2012,* part 1, 447–61.

Hughes, Christopher (2003) Fighting the smokeless war. In Hughes, C. R. and Wacker, G., *China and the Internet: Politics of the Digital Leap Forward.* Routledge, London, 139–61.

Hunton & Williams LLP (2013a) Chinese legislature passes data privacy resolution. Blog, 2 January. http://www.huntonprivacyblog.com/2013/01/articles/chinese-legislature-passes-data-privacy-resolution.

Hunton & Williams LLP (2013b) Chinese Ministry of Industry and Information Technology enacts new data protection rule. Blog, 26 July. http://www.huntonprivacyblog.com/2013/07/articles/chinese-ministry-of-industry-and-information-technology-enacts-new-data-protection-rule.

Hwang Ji-Jen (2012) *China's Cyber Warfare: The Strategic Value of Cyberspace and the Legacy of People's War.* PhD thesis, Newcastle University.

Inkster, Nigel (2010) China in cyber space. *Survival,* 52(4), 55–66.

Intelligence Squared Debate (2010) The cyber war threat has been grossly exaggerated. 8 June, transcript, p. 7. http://intelligencesquaredus.org/wp-content/uploads/Cyber-War-060810.pdf.

ITU (2013) *Measuring the Information Society 2013.* ITU, Geneva. http://www.itu.int/en/ITU-D/Statistics/Documents/publications/mis2013/MIS2013_without_Annex_4.pdf.

Ji Ping (2011) Implementing higher education quality assurance on system level: The case of China. Presented at the Asia Europe Meeting (ASEM) Bonn. http://www.asem-education-secretariat.org/imperia/md/content/asem2/events/2011asemqaseminar/4_jiping.pdf.

Jiang Zemin (2010) *On the Development of China's Information Technology Industry,* trans. Central Party Literature Press and Shanghai Jiao Tong

University Press. Elsevier, Oxford. [First published in Chinese (2009). Central Party Literature Press and Shanghai Jiatong University Press.]

King, Gary, Pan, Jennifer and Roberts, Margaret E. (2013) How censorship in China allows government criticism but silences collective expression. *American Political Science Review*, May. http://gking.harvard.edu/files/gking/files/censored.pdf.

Kirkman, Geoffrey, Cornelius, Peter K., Sachs, Jeffrey D. and Schwab, Klaus (eds.) (2002) *The Global Information Technology Report 2001–2002: Readiness for the Networked World*. Oxford University Press, Oxford.

Krekel, Bryan, Adams, Patton and Bakos, George (2012) Occupying the information high ground: Chinese capabilities for computer network operations and cyber espionage. Prepared for the U.S.–China Economic and Security Review Commission by Northrop Grumman Corp. http://www.gwu.edu/~nsarchiv/NSAEBB/NSAEBB424/docs/Cyber-066.pdf.

Krepinevich, Andrew (2012) *Cyber Warfare: A 'Nuclear Option'?* Center for Budgetary Assessments, Washington DC.

Laforet, Sylvie (2009) Chinese consumers' attitudes and adoption of online and mobile banking. In de Pablos, P. O. and Lytras, M. D. (eds.), *The China Information Technology Handbook*. Springer, Dordrecht, 23–40.

Lai, David (2010) Introduction. In Kamphausen, R., Lai, D. and Scobell, A. (eds.), *The PLA at Home and Abroad: Assessing the Operational Capabilities of China's Military*. US Army War College Press, Carlisle PA, 1–44.

Leu, Russell (2013) China's first-ever national standard on data privacy: Best practices for companies. In China on Managing Data Privacy: China Law Update. Blog, 13 June. http://www.chinalawupdate.cn/2013/06/articles/other/chinas-firstever-national-standard-on-data-privacy-best-practices-for-companies-in-china-on-managing-data-privacy.

Lewis, James A. (2005) Computer espionage, Titan Rain and China. Center for Strategic and International Studies – Technology and Public Policy Program, December. http://csis.org/files/media/csis/pubs/051214_china_titan_rain.pdf.

Li Guojie (ed.) (2011) *Information Science and Technology in China: A Roadmap to 2050*. Chinese Academy of Social Sciences/Science Press/Springer, Beijing.

Li Haizheng (2011) Higher education in China: Complement or competition to US universities? In Clotfelter, C. T. (ed.), *American Universities in a Global Market*. National Bureau of Economic Research, University of Chicago Press, Chicago, 269–304.

Li Xiaodong (2012) The Western theories of war ethics and contemporary controversies. http://english.cssn.cn/8203/820305/201202/t20120225_23 1239.shtml.

Li Zhongzhou (2006) China's informatization strategy and its impact on trade in ICT goods and ICT services. Presented at the UNCTAD Expert Meeting in Support of the Implementation and Follow-Up of WSIS: Using ICTs to Achieve Growth and Development, jointly organized by UNCTAD, OECD and ILO, 4–5 December. http://archive.unctad.org/sections/wcmu/docs/c3em29p016_en.pdf.

Lieberthal, Kenneth (2004) *Governing China: From Revolution through Reform* (2nd edition). W. W. Norton, New York.

Lieberthal, Kenneth and Oksenberg, Michael (1988) *Policy Making in China: Leaders, Structures and Processes*. Princeton University Press, Princeton NJ.

Ling Lan (2005) Enhancing e-democracy via fiscal transparency: A discussion based on China's experience. In Böhlen, M., Gamper, J., Polasek, W. and Wimmer, M. A. (eds.), *E-Government: Towards Electronic Democracy*. Proceedings of the International Conference TCGOV 2005, Bolzano, Italy, 2–4 March. Springer, Berlin/Heidelberg/New York, 57–69.

Liu Chun (2012) The myth of informatization in rural areas: The case of China's Sichuan province. *Government Information Quarterly*, 29(1), 85–97.

Livingston, Scott (2013) China releases national standard for personal information collected over information systems; industry self-regulatory organization established. *Inside Privacy*, 25 January. http://www.insideprivacy.com/international/china-releases-national-standard-for-personal-information-collected-over-information-systems-industr.

Lü Yao-Huai (2005) Privacy and data privacy issues in contemporary China. *Ethics and Information Technology*, 7, 7–15.

Ma Lie (2012) Call for information security law. *China Daily*.com, 6 March.

McGregor, James (2010) *China's Drive for 'Indigenous Innovation': A Web of Industrial Policies*. Global Intellectual Property Center/U.S. Chamber of Commerce/APCO Worldwide. https://www.uschamber.com/sites/default/files/legacy/reports/100728chinareport_0.pdf.

Machlup, Fritz (1962) *The Production and Distribution of Knowledge in the United States*. Princeton University Press, Princeton NJ.

MacKinnon, Rebecca (2011) China's 'networked authoritarianism'. *Journal of Democracy*, 22(2), 32–46.

MANDIANT (2013) *APT1: Exposing One of China's Cyber Espionage Units*. www.mandiant.com.

Masuda, Yoneji (1981 [1980]) *The Information Society as Post-Industrial Society*. World Future Society, Bethesda MD.

Mattis, Peter (2013) Informatization drives expanded scope of public security. *China Brief*, 13(8), 12 April. http://www.jamestown.org/single/?no_cache =1&tx_ttnews[tt_news]=40721#.UbHkMpzleSo.

Mattis, Peter (2011) China's adaptive approach to the information counter-revolution. *China Brief*, 11(10), 3 June. http://www.jamestown. org/single/?no_cache=1&tx_ttnews[tt_news]=38013&tx_ttnews [backPid]=517#.UbHn3JzleSo.

Meltzer, Joshua (2013) *Taiwan's Economic Opportunities and Challenges and the Importance of the Trans-Pacific Partnership.* Working Paper, Brookings Institution, Washington DC.

Meng Qingxuan and Li Mingzhi (2001) *New Economy and ICT Development in China.* WIDER Discussion Papers, World Institute for Development Economics (UNUWIDER), 2001/76. http://hdl.handle.net/10419/53080.

Minzer, Carl (2010) *Countries at the Crossroads 2011: China.* Freedom House. http://www.freedomhouse.org/sites/default/files/inline_images/China FINAL.pdf.

Moran, Theodore H. (2011) *Foreign Manufacturing Multinationals and the Transformation of the Chinese Economy: New Measurements, New Perspectives.* Working Paper, Petersen Institute for International Economics, Washington DC, April.

Mueller, Milton and Lovelock, Peter (2000) The WTO and China's ban on foreign investment in telecommunication services: A game-theoretic analysis. *Telecommunications Policy*, 24(8–9), 731–59.

Mulvenon, James (2009) Chairman Hu and the PLA's 'new historic mission'. *China Leadership Monitor*, 27. http://media.hoover.org/sites/default/files/ documents/CLM27JM.pdf.

Mulvenon, James (2008) 'True is false, false is true, virtual is reality, reality is virtual': Technology and simulation in the Chinese military training revolution. In Kamphausen, R., Scobell, A. and Tanner, T. (eds.), *The 'People' in the PLA: Recruitment, Training, and Education in China's Military.* United States Army Strategic Studies Institute, Carlisle PA, 49–98. http:// www.strategicstudiesinstitute.army.mil/pdffiles/pub858.pdf.

Mulvenon, James (1999) The PLA and information warfare. In Mulvenon, J. C. and Yang, R. H. (eds.), *The People's Liberation Army in the Information Age.* Rand, Santa Monica CA, 175–86.

National Research Council (2012) *The New Global Ecosystem in Advanced Computing: Implications for U.S. Competitiveness and National Security.* Committee on Global Approaches to Advanced Computing, Board on Global Science and Technology; Policy and Global Affairs Division. National Academies Press, Washington DC.

ONCIX (US Office of the National Counterintelligence Executive) (2011) *Foreign Spies Stealing US Economic Secrets in Cyberspace: Report to Congress on Foreign Economic Collection and Industrial Espionage, 2009–2011.* October. http://www.ncix.gov/publications/reports/fecie_all/Foreign_Economic _Collection_2011.pdf.

Orcutt, John and Shen Hong (2010) *Shaping China's Innovation Future: University Technology Transfer in Transition.* Edward Elgar, Cheltenham.

Polpetter, Kevin (2010) Towards an integrative C4ISR system: Informationization and joint operations in the People's Liberation Army. In Kamphausen, R., Lai, D. and Scobell A. (eds.), *The PLA at Home and Abroad: Assessing the Operational Capabilities of China's Military.* US Army War College Press, Carlisle PA, 193–236.

Qiang, Christine Zhen-Wei (2007) *China's Information Revolution: Managing the Economic and Social Transformation.* World Bank, Washington DC.

Qiang, Christine Zhen-Wei, Bhavnani, Asheeta, Hanna, Nagy K., Kimura, Kaoru and Sudan, Randeep (2009) *Rural Informatization in China.* World Bank, Washington DC.

Qin Gang (2007) China's malformed media sphere. *China Media Project,* Hong Kong University, 11 July. http://cmp.hku.hk/2012/07/11/25293.

Qu Weizhi (2010) *China's Path to Informatization,* English edn. Cengage Learning Asia, Hong Kong.

Ramzy, A. (2011) Wired up. *Time Magazine,* 17 February. http://www. time.com/time/magazine/article/0,9171,2048171,00.html#ixzz2Vd0gw UXk.

Rauscher, Karl Frederick and Zhou Yonglin (2013) *Frank Communication and Sensible Cooperation to Stop Harmful Hacking.* EastWest Institute and Internet Society of China. http://www.cert.org.cn/publish/main/upload/File/China-U.S.%20Anti-Hacking%20Report%20v190.pdf.

RFA (Radio Free Asia) (2012) Lecturer sent to mental hospital. Radio Free Asia, 11 December. http://www.rfa.org/english/news/china/sent-1211201215 0340.html.

Scobell, Andrew (2010) Discourse in 3-D: The PLA's evolving doctrine, circa 2009. In Kamphausen, R., Lai, D. and Scobell, A. (eds.), *The PLA at Home and Abroad: Assessing the Operational Capabilities of China's Military.* US Army War College Press, Carlisle PA, 99–134.

Segal, Adam (2012) The cyber trade war. *Foreign Policy,* 25 October. http://www. cfr.org/cybersecurity/cyber-trade-war/p29356?cid=emc-ACC_Spring13_ BCK-Segal_Cyber_Trade_War-042513.

Serger, Sylvia and Breidne, Magnus (2007) China's fifteen year plan for science and technology: An assessment. *Asia Policy,* 1(4), 135–64.

Sha Zukang (2002) Statement by Ambassador Sha Zukang, Head of the Chinese Delegation at the First Meeting of the Intergovernmental Preparatory Committee of the World Summit on the Information Society, 1 July, Geneva. http://www.fmprc.gov.cn/eng/wjdt/zyjh/t25077.htm.

Simon, Denis Fred and Cao Cong (2009) *China's Technological Edge: Assessing the Role of High-end Talent*. Cambridge University Press, Cambridge.

SIPO (2008) Outline of the National Intellectual Property Strategy (issued by the State Council of the People's Republic of China on 25 June). http://www.wipo.int/wipolex/en/details.jsp?id=859.

Snell, Robin and Tseng Choo Sin (2002) Moral atmosphere and moral influence under China's network capitalism. *Organization Studies*, 23, 449–78.

Springut, Micah, Schlaijker, Stephen and Chen, David (2011) *China's Program for Science and Technology Modernization: Implications for American Competitiveness*. Prepared for the U.S.–China Economic and Security Review Commission. CENTRA Technology, Arlington VA.

Suttmeier, Richard P. and Shi Bing (2008) Success in 'Pasteur's quadrant'? The Chinese Academy of Sciences and its role in the National Innovation System. In Rowen, H. S., Gong Hancock, M. and Miller, W. F. (eds.), *Greater China's Quest for Innovation*. Walter H. Shorenstein Asia Pacific Research Center, Stanford CA, 35–56.

Tanyildiz, Zeynep Esra (2013) The ethnic composition of science and engineering research laboratories in the United States. *International Migration*, 28 January. http://onlinelibrary.wiley.com/doi/10.1111/imig.12035/pdf.

Tendulkar, Rohini (2013) *Cyber-Crime, Securities Markets and Systemic Risk*. Joint Staff Working Paper of the International Organization of Securities Commissions and World Federation of Exchanges, 16 July. http://www.world-exchanges.org/files/statistics/pdf/IOSCO_WFE_Cyber-crime%20report_Final_16July.pdf.

Toffler, Alvin (1980) *The Third Wave*. Bantam Books, New York.

Tung, Rosalie L. (2008). Brain circulation, diaspora, and international competitiveness. *European Management Journal*, 26, 298–304.

USCBC (US–China Business Council) (2009) *Request for Company Input on PRC Domestic Innovation Policies*. US-China Business Council, 15 December. http://cbi.typepad.com/files/us-china-business-council—indigenous-innovation-policy-brief-1.pdf.

Vogel, Ezra (2011) *Deng Xiaoping and the Transformation of China*. Belknap Press, Cambridge MA.

Wacker, Gudrun (2003) The internet and censorship in China. In Hughes, C. and Wacker, G. (eds.), *China and the Internet: Politics of the Digital Leap Forward*. Routledge Curzon, London, 58–82.

Wang Hao (2011) *Protecting Privacy in China*. Springer, Heidelberg.

Wang Qun (2011) Speech by H.E. Ambassador Wang Qun at the First Committee of the 66th Session of the GA on Information and Cyberspace Security, 20 October. http://www.fmprc.gov.cn/eng/wjdt/zyjh/t869580.htm.

Wang Wensheng, Peng Guangqian and Lu Guangming (2009) Agricultural informationization in China. In de Pablos, P. O. and Lytras, M. D. (eds.), *The China Information Technology Handbook*. Springer, Dordrecht, 271–97.

Wang Xinjun (2012) China makes military budget based on strict principles. China Military News cited from *People's Daily Overseas Edition*, 6 March. http://www.china-defense-mashup.com/china-makes-military-budget-based-on-strict-principles.html.

Webster, Frank (2006) *Theories of the Information Society* (3rd edition) Routledge, Oxford.

WEF and INSEAD (2013) *The Global Information Technology Report 2013*. WEF, Geneva. http://www.weforum.org/reports/global-information-technology-report-2013.

WEF and INSEAD (2012) *The Global Information Technology Report 2012*. WEF, Geneva. http://www.weforum.org/reports/global-information-technology-report-2012.

WEF and INSEAD (2011) *The Global Information Technology Report 2010–2011*. WEF, Geneva. http://www3.weforum.org/docs/WEF_GITR_Report_2011.pdf.

Wei Jingsheng (1978) The Fifth Modernization. In translation, http://www.rjgeib.com/thoughts/china/jingshen.html.

Wiener, Norbert (1964) *God & Golem, Inc.: A Comment on Certain Points where Cybernetics Impinges on Religion*. MIT Press, Cambridge MA.

WIP (World Internet Project) (2009) *World Internet Project International Report 2009*. http://www.digitalcenter.org/wp-content/uploads/2013/02/WIP-report-2009-final.pdf.

WOIPFG (World Organization to Investigate the Persecution of Falun Gong) (2005) *Investigation on Microsoft's Involvement in the Chinese Communist Party's Human Rights Abuses*. August. http://www.upholdjustice.org/node/156.

World Bank (2001) *China and the Knowledge Economy: Seizing the 21st Century*. World Bank, Washington, DC. http://info.worldbank.org/etools/docs/library/137742/ChinaKE.pdf.

World Bank (2000) *China's Development Strategy: The Knowledge and Innovation Perspective*. World Bank, Washington DC. http://info.worldbank.org/etools/docs/library/108303/ChinaDevStrat.pdf.

World Bank and DRC (Development Research Center of the State Council, People's Republic of China) (2012) *China 2030: Building a Modern, Harmonious, and Creative High-Income Society*. Conference edn. http://www-wds.worldbank.org/external/default/WDSContentServer/WDSP/IB/2012/02/28/000356161_20120228001303/Rendered/PDF/671790WP0P127500China020300complete.pdf.

Wu Bangguo (2011) Report on the work of the Standing Committee of the National People's Congress. Delivered at the Fourth Session of the Eleventh National People's Congress, 10 March. http://english.gov.cn/official/2011-03/18/content_1827230.htm.

Xia Jun (2010) Linking ICTs to rural development: China's rural information policy. *Government Information Quarterly*, 27(2), 187–95.

Xiao Weibing (2012) *Freedom of Information Reform in China: Information Flow Analysis*. Routledge, London.

Xu Chuan-xiang (2004) *National Informatization Index System of China*. http://www.cicc.or.jp/japanese/kouryu/pdf_ppt/04china.pdf.

Xue Lan and Liang Zheng (2008) Multinational R&D in China: Myths and realities. In Rowen, H. S., Hancock, M. and Miller, W. F. (eds.), *Greater China's Quest for Innovation*. Walter H. Shorenstein Asia-Pacific Research Center Books, Stanford CA, 103–22.

Yang Fengchun (2009) The style and contents of China government in steering eGovernment construction and implementation. In Jirapon Tubtimhin and Pipe, R. (eds.), *Global E-Governance: Advancing E-Governance through Innovation and Leadership*. IOS Press, Amsterdam, 84–93.

Yang Rui (2005) Toward massification: Higher education development in the People's Republic of China since 1949. In Smart, J. C. (ed.), *Higher Education: Handbook of Theory and Research*, vol. 19. Springer, Dordrecht, 311–74.

Yang Rui (2002) *Third Delight: The Internationalization of Higher Education in China*. Routledge, Abingdon.

Yang Su (2011) *Collective Killings in Rural China during the Cultural Revolution*. Cambridge University Press, Cambridge.

Yi Wenli (2012) Divergence and co-operation between China and the U.S. on the cyberspace issue. *Contemporary International Relations*, 4, 124–41.

Yu Hua (2012) *China in Ten Words*, trans. Alan H. Barr. Vintage, New York.

Zeng Haijun, Huang Ronghuai, Zhao Yuchi and Zhang Jinbao (2012) *ICT and ODL in Education for Rural Development: Current Situation and Good Practices in China*. http://www.inruled.org/iERD/Publication/iERD%20in%20China%20for%20eLA%20%28UNESCO-INRULED%29.pdf.

Zeng Shaojun (2010) Searching for disappeared trust in China: With a discussion of Prof. W. F. Tang's *Public Opinion & Political Change in China. China Nonprofit Review*, 2(2), 363–75.

Zha Qiang and Li Jun with Cheng Xiaofang (2011) The University of Science and Technology of China: Can the Caltech model take root in Chinese soil? In Hayhoe, R., Li Jun, Lin Jing and Zha Qiang, *Portraits of 21st Century Chinese Universities: In the Move to Mass Higher Education.* Springer, Dordrecht, 271–306.

Zhang Fanghua and Tao Jingyuan (2012) Study on relationship among FDI's spillover, intellectual capital and innovation capability in China. *2012 Second International Conference on Business Computing and Global Informatization*, 943–46.

Zhao Yuezhi (2008) *Communication in China: Political Economy, Power, and Conflict.* Rowman and Littlefield, Lanham MD.

Zhao Ziyang (2009) *Prisoner of the State: The Secret Journal of Zhao Ziyang*, trans. and ed. Bao Pu, Renee Chiang and Adi Ignatius. Simon & Schuster, New York.

Zheng Silin and Ward, Michael R. (2011) The effects of market liberalization and privatization on Chinese telecommunications. *China Economic Review*, 22(2), 210–20.

Zhi Xiaoli and Gao Fuping (2008) Improving the regulative environment to facilitate the exploitation of information resources in the People's Republic of China. In Fitzgerald, B., Gao, F., O'Brien, D. and Shi, S. X. (eds.), *Copyright Law, Digital Content and the Internet in the Asia-Pacific.* Sydney University Press, Sydney, 155–69.

Zhu Tao, Phipps, David, Pridgen, Adam, Crandall, Jedidiah R. and Wallach, Dan S. (2013) The velocity of censorship: High-fidelity detection of microblog post deletions. Cornell University Library. Submitted 4 March, arXiv:1303.0597v1 [cs.IR]. http://arxiv.org/abs/1303.0597.

Index